Silk City

I Shall Not Want...

Brunilda Milan©

Silk City

Silk City®
Milan Publisher
ISBN-13:
978-0615591889 (Milan Publisher)

ISBN-10:
0615591884

brunildamilan.com

Genre: Novel
Category: Spiritual Growth

"I can do every-thing through him who gives me strength."

Philippians 4:13

Silk City

Table of Contents

●●●

Prologue

"All man's ways seem innocent to him, but motives are weighted by the Lord." Proverbs 16:2

The unique story developed within the historical background flair on a city known by many as, *"Silk City."* The story saturated with childhood memories inspired and safeguarded by Rose Marie, helped deal with growing pains. The teenage girl lived placid in a slow pace Tropical Island, then moved unexpectedly to a cosmopolitan fast growing city; Paterson, New Jersey. Constantly, she compared the island and the city, until both, became very important elements throughout her fragile life.

The story narrated retrospectively by Rose Marie's during childhood sequenced into the unforgettable, turmoil high school years, which gave clear insights on the adulthood struggles. Rose Marie learned to fight back, after numerous confrontations, victimized by the language and cultural limitations. She was pushed into appalled limits via ruthless bullies, heightened by detrimental parent relationship, surrounded by other unbearable circumstances. At times, sustained only by God's grace when she repeatedly was assaulted verbally, humiliated and labeled, *"Newcomer, Spick, and Four Eyes."* Intentionally, the despicable negative connotations misled others about her true personality. Names well known by many that arrived from other countries and tried their luck in the city.

The *Newcomer* desperately attempted to find harmony with the only familiar thread available throughout nature. However, the memorable Great Falls Park served as a peaceful place, where she could find fountain fresh pure air breath in the midst of an over-populated smog city. The young girl frantically reached for support to the multicultural people already familiarized with local customs. Instead, the Newcomer found similar problems overwhelmed and were barely unable to handle. Rose Marie surrounded by total indifference felt an unbearable painful loneliness. Eventually, she ended with a heavy burden broken heart.

Meanwhile the Newcomer guided by instincts found consolation, refuge, and inspiration from childhood memories back home in the island. Rose Marie desperately kept unsettled dreams deep desires secretive buried, though they constantly burn inside her heart. After all, Rose Marie entrusted God with all desires and dreams, guided by hope, since one day would fulfill and accomplish soul purpose at heart.

Nevertheless, Silk City ruthless reputation could not be easily ignore and made arrogant scars impression in the girl's mind. As time, passed Rose Marie's character strength grew stronger tested repeatedly the drilled phrase: *"Only the strong survived."* She believed God's Word learned as a child put to test as a youth:

"You are my lamp oh Lord, the Lord turns my darkness into light." *2 Samuel 22:29* ●●●

Dedication

"Trust in the Lord with all your heart and lean not on your own understanding: in all your ways acknowledge him, and he will make paths straight."
Proverbs 3:5-6(RV)

To all parents that made many sacrifices for their children's best interest!

To my loving, father *Dionisio Milan,* often called *Dominick,* spent most of his lifetime as a worker at a chemical plant. In return, he acquired a long-term lung disease, due to the improper protection and unsafe work environment. He striven simply to bring bread to the family of six children. He wanted them to have comfortable descent life, even through his personal expense.

Nora Anazagasty a beloved virtuous mother who raised six children, fourteen grandchildren, and twelve great–great grandchildren. Nora was an innocent unknowingly participant, victim of social and economic detrimental circumstances.

Regardless, both parents believed in their children strong values through education during precarious times. Parents taught God's love and values to struggle even against the odds to achieved the American dream. Thanks to both!

From my heart with love,

Brunilda Milan

●●●

Paterson, New Jersey

Chapter 1

CONSCIOUSNESS STREAM...

*"For a man's ways are in full view of the Lord,
and he examines all his paths." Proverbs 5:21*

Rose Marie walked briskly down the familiar streets and took heavy steps towards the Paterson Historic Museum, located on the Historic Trail Ways, at Market Street. Rose Marie wanted desperately arrive just before closing time. She walked swiftly stretched her legs, as far as possible. The arms swung forcefully side-by-side to beat the strong wind thrust, typical weather on a spring afternoon.

Rose Marie made up her mind, *"I must beat the unstoppable clock and reach the Museum before it closed."*

Further down the corner, between Main and Grand Street, Rose Marie could see the splendorous seventeen century Gothic church structure. Unmistakably, St. John Cathedral was the city's architectural jewel enhanced dramatically the area. The high tower protuberance overlooked vigilant the downtown area. The Cathedral majestically displayed an enormous clock seen from blocks away. At the distant, Garret Mountains silhouette mystically embellished the horizon clearly contrasted with the city. The two faded white stone lions roared the city's entrance, guarded historical relics at Lambert Castle Historic Museum. The castle gave a rich flamboyant testimonial of flourished times during past generations.

Rose Marie passed Main Street towards Market St. *"Some things never changed,"* she thought then continued down the crowded streets.

"Always the tedious heavy traffic between good old faithful Market and Spruce Streets," she smiled and moved pass everyone.

Then, Rose Marie darted across the wide avenue full of pedestrians, crossed the green light, like everyone else before it changed to red.

Rose Marie steered clearly away from the downtown packed sidewalk sales with curious shoppers frantically looked for bargains; a reflection of harsh times, in the city. After a moment, she took a shortcut at the narrow path by the small brook behind, Van Houten Street. Then, she walked towards the newly renovated brick apartment buildings.

Finally, Rose Marie arrived to a specific renovated mill building. The wide glass museum doors displayed a common red sign, *"Welcome,"* faded by direct sun rays, which bombarded constantly the entrance.

Rose Marie glanced excitedly, *"still an hour before close time."*

She smiled and felt victoriously, *"At least this time, I won the race against the clock."*

It took many years, before Rose Marie gathered enough courage returned fearless to the familiar brick buildings, once dreadfully dark humid mills. Many mills surrounded the Great Falls areas beamed with productive manufacture plants during the textile era. Afterwards, the lack of textile productivity and rundown buildings became abandon and useless. Many factors, accelerated the deterioration at the abandoned mills. The inclement weather, plus poor maintenance conditions accelerated the process. Furthermore, youth loitering, improvised shelters for those homeless and increase numbers of drug addicts' used the empty buildings for temporary relief and shelter. Besides, the governmental plain indifference were among the many factors for the fast deterioration.

Finally, there was a change of heart after many years of abandonment. The buildings were rescued from ruins and restored by the city's historic conservation and restoration policies. Once again, the mills restored to their maximum splendor finally occupied for different purposes.

A Christian private school was among the first to jump into the newly renovated buildings. Other mills, became living quarters for middle class income families. Furthermore, the strategic Market and Mill Street, a spacious brick mill, became proud new home of the city's Museum historic valuable treasures. The Paterson Historic Museum safeguarded patriotic founder city history and all the facets historic pilgrimage adventures. Besides, it sheltered important inventions in the city that benefit the country. Mostly, the Museum recollected evidence how the textiles revolutionized the world by the Industrial Revolution.

Rose Marie walked inside the Museum absorbed by an exuberant trance at each detail. Surprisingly, she remembered exactly where everything throughout the long galleries were located at the main gallery. Rose Marie walked directly towards a unique gallery. She stood quietly for a few endless minutes, observed pale the shiny impeccable glass window her reflection.

"Definitely, in my opinion, this particular gallery is by far more the core attraction in the entire museum."

Rose Marie embellished and wrapped in her inner feelings, knew it was her favorite exhibition, *"Oh, priceless history treasures, richer than gemstones,"* she said almost in a whisper.

Rose Marie scrutinized carefully up and down the priceless exhibition. She stood motionless almost paralyzed in fearful admiration felt once again goose bumps on her neck!

Nevertheless, she wondered how popular silk became the city's name after silk production. Among the glass, displayed a few practical silky soft attires. Definitely, the items caught visitors eyes reflected appropriately the raw silk mercantile period at the vivid colorful city. The textile era, moved the city and the country's economy to unimaginable high levels. The silk expansion motivated both rapid growth in city's wealth and great work attraction for many people of different backgrounds.

The refine silky household items produced by useful versatile silk gave city its preponderance name, *"Silk City."* Rose Marie knew the silk era exposed important details on city's development into grand proportions finally acquired the name recognition!

Silk City

As a result, both the country and urban city rapidly developed an uncontested account on the ever lasted history during earlier eras. In 1800's, *Silk City,* produced half of America's silk. The Industrial revolution led into unimaginable city rapid demographic and economical growth. During the industrial revolution, the city mainly manufactured almost all the silk textiles goods. Silk was indispensable for household garments, too.

Who could think from something ugly, small somehow repulsive despite most human eyes, came something especially beautiful, worthy and transcendental. Soft silky fabrics became useful to man approved and stamped by the test of time.

Rose Marie observed silently the raw silk process paraded softly in front. Even so, most people at the Museum probably ignored the tedious process took to obtain beautiful silk for textiles. Where did silk come from? Many questions came to her mind. Why was a young girl fascinated with soft gentle silk? Therefore, Rose Marie observed the raw silk stages and compared parallel periods during younger years. For a glimpse seconds, unwillingly without expected retort the young girl hung head shamefully, just as those teenage years. Rose Marie thought, *"Silk and I have so many similarities."*

Rose Marie wondered about teen years were long gone. Surely, *"I was a miserable teenager, a lost soul at the city,"* she mumbled.

Suddenly, those inevitable chaotic years pounded loudly in her head. Rose Marie recognized the unfortunate chaos during her youthful years. Silk reflected instinctively horrible turmoil years lived in the city. *"Many times, I felt ugly, unwanted and useless, like the despicable silkworm."*

Silk came from common silkworms' creatures grown in farms. Simple insects, apparently most people could care less, had a special purpose, produce silk! Farms produced silkworms until it reached cocoon larva rudimentary stage and then extracted the silk. Nevertheless, those repulsive hardy creatures had a singular job production of the finest silk known to mankind, fit for Emperors and Kings! An ultimate reward, bestowed worms by nature itself! For a moment, Rose Marie sighted uncomfortable, *"God, how I felt so insignificant back those days!"* The reminiscences asleep for a long time by the inner self-defense mechanism, buried in the sub-conscious, had suddenly awoke. Something, insignificantly small, as a silkworm, abruptly awoke the essence of all. Rose Marie defenseless without energy or knowledge to fight back during those adolescence perplexed times. Why?

Rose Marie clenched fist tightly walked through the museum's galleries to forget. Why did she come back to the city that cause so much pain? Indeed, Rose Marie controlled emotions not to call attention to others,which strolled in fascination down the galleries as they glimpsed history unfolded magically in front of their eyes. Rose Marie's guts, revolted quickly, as if a centrifuge, deep emotions escaped clearly to the surface.

She looked carefully around to see if someone noticed the uncontrollable cry sensations. Meanwhile, visitors were so mesmerized by the attractive displays paid little or no attention to the relentless woman walked around the gallery. Meanwhile, memories emerged one by one; unable to stop tears ran freely down her cheeks.

Eventually, Rose Marie passed visitors, as expressions turned grin into a fake smile. She compelled weak smiles to hide the pain. *"Hurts to smile."* Rose Marie fought against buried images emerged dismay. Gentle, as if a lost lonely child, sobbed quietly into the next exhibition.

She denied for the longest time, thoughts from cruel episodes at the famous city and thought, *"whao, still so much pain."* As a child, Biblical stories kept her from given exactly into the same concepts: inadequacy, shame, and ugliness.

Furthermore, to make matters worse, Rose Marie's memories triggered empty love phrases from the soft elevator music in the background. Suddenly, she remembered peaceful ambiance brought by the soft music found in Rose Marie's favorite place back in the island. Persistent soft music, invited body and soul trust love, again. The music harmonized with the Museum's ambience clearly an invitation to relax. *"Good old sixties love songs followed by the unforgettable seventies, were almost a soft whisper."*

Nevertheless, songs written in love's name were like a heavy hammer in the hands of an apprentice carpenter, which build no matter the outcome. Rose Marie preferred selective forgetfulness, but life intended deliberately remember each occurrence in the big city.

Rose Marie needed an escape from it all. Suddenly, she redirected interest upwards. She strolled by large images, a sharp contrast with the Museum's white walls. The newly grand exhibition displayed oversized posters based on priceless Silk City's textiles immigrant workers. The men and women unknown faces behind textile machinery, represented hard workers immigrants' era ranged intriguingly throughout the museum.

"A picture is worth a thousand words," she thought. Nameless immigrants' photographs reflected vividly the different facets to their lives, some happiness, but others painful struggles. Some images were emotionally cold and distant. While, others reflected tired faces from cold rusted machinery period, once ruled famous Silk City. Some, reflected sweet smiley faces eager workers satisfied with their destiny. These immigrants wrote the city's history full of dreams and desires burst at the seams ready to tackle the world. Others, looked solemnly tired with certain toughness in their eyes. Perhaps, others cast lonely painful shadows, full of sorrows away from home and love ones, dictated by ultimate textile end.

These people suffered immense pains similar in many ways to the *"Newcomers."* They came through *Ellis Island* in *New York City*, where there was no turning back. The relocation process began indifferently to pain, personal sorrows, or expectations. Hundreds fluctuated into Silk City and nearby cities for different textiles jobs. Many courageous immigrants shared common stories when they left behind their country, homes, and love ones.

Regardless the outcomes, they justified pain by deep desires to seek freedom, to find better economic conditions, and improve social opportunities at the new country. The Newcomer felt akin with images on the walls. The images held together by strong upbringings and family ties under strenuous circumstances. *"Excruciating agonizing survival tales,"* Rose Marie thought sadly. Rose Marie recognized those frighten thoughts, too. They shared common inexperience at the unknown culture, as they left their countries behind. Many, overwhelmed by the exodus experience, changed completely their life's outlook just as once, Rose Marie.

Memorable historic city, flocked people together from different cultural backgrounds and produced textiles eventually turned city's industrial outlook. Regardless, conditions hard workers immigrants managed to leave footprints that built city's earlier manufacture era. Also, the Passaic River played an important element for silk development. Nevertheless, history's ark treasurers gave due credits to Silk production and immigrants; both important elements, built *Silk City* to its fullest potentials.

It was almost closing time, Rose Marie flowed right into the final gallery. The last exhibition caught her undivided attention. In 1775, thundering black powder war, marked the country's beginnings. The Revolutionary War reenactment the last battle scene with miniature soldiers and rustic weapons, were quite a sight! Rose Marie visualized the colonies during Revolutionary War united to create a new country. She thought how, *"First, the colonies*

[17]

materialized needy desires for independence in their minds." Immediately, the independence plans went into action. Indeed, the Newcomer understood clearly the battles fought first in colonies' minds. Then, their strong patriotic sense led to the ultimatum freedom to obtain victory goals! Events that followed brew to boiling point exploded into actions, just like during her teenage years. Thus, colonies eventually won independence, the same as Rose Marie.

For a moment, Rose Marie thought how difficult teenage years were the same as Colonial times. Rose Marie chose simple weapons stored in the mind and fought her own wars. Childhood fond memories shield Rose Marie's loneliness in such swarm city. Rose Marie remembered first spiritual warfare dealt with the exodus pain, as she left behind love ones and friends at the beloved Island.

On the other hand, the island set boundaries for the young Latina and kept shield from the real world. Suddenly, the last straw changed drastically during unforgettable sixties altered Rose Marie's life. The Dad; head of the family, imposed his authority with the best interest in heart and family well-being during difficult economic times. He announced without hesitation:

"We are leaving the island in a few months."

Unspeakable feelings emerged, while unknown boundaries were set without questions. Rose Marie at a vulnerable age thirteen, prime youth, became one more resident in the hasty city, a complete stranger without friends or loves ones. Subsequently, Rose Marie during her best teenage years, when was time laugh and cry of joy, facts remained turbulent, unease, and full of despair. Instead, Rose Marie turned quickly mature mostly out of despair, without time to assimilate the cultural shock. The abrupt changes smashed unmercifully Rose Marie's self-esteem, changed her personality and killed the hopes to become an actress, one day. The city looked harsh meaningless in the outside resembled the silkworm cocoons. Meanwhile, the Newcomer remained sensitive, soft, and gentle inside, as the finest silk. Afterward, Rose Marie developed in God's due time, but not before she paid a high painful price throughout the acculturation process.

Rose Marie looked back at youthful years gone a long time ago. Lost times, Newcomer discovered the hardest way gentleness was a sign unacceptable at the city. Such aggressive environment saw weakness as wimps' misfits. Rose Marie became tougher, assertive, and joined the mainstream rough majority in order to survive.

Finally, Rose Marie's survival instincts took over both outcomes; good and bad. Rose Marie remembered survival came by pure heritage instincts learned from grandma's Indian ancestral heritage. The Latina girl quenched pain with childhood memories, which brought peace and calmness during tough moments at the city. Sometimes, Rose Marie drifted away to the island, so pain became less, almost unimportant.

After a while, Rose Marie discovered no one could take away precious significant moments from childhood memories. Moments, lived at the island could not erase easily, since were recollected already in the subconscious. Memories fought against desperation and inadequacy felt just right. Rose Marie recalled, *"Sustained by God's love, never failed."* She recognized, *"God's unconditional love."* She learned to go with the flow, *"Always God was available just in time, like a lifesaver."*

Indeed, it took long to understand the power in properly chosen memories provided an escape vehicle. Afterwards, memories served as a healing bridge with parents' broken relationship and came to terms with parents. Finally, she broke chains free and forgave one another. Most of all, Rose Marie broke self-pity inadequacy bondage and came out from self-inflicted cocoon, entrusted God all Mighty! Rose Marie fought hard equipped with God's Word s to conquer the big city. This time, she was not alone!

"Commit to the lord whatever you do and your plans will succeed." Proverbs 16:3

●●●

Chapter 2

STORY TO TELL

*"Heaven and earth will pass away, but my words
will never pass away."*
Mathew 24:35

Rose Marie discovered her mission in life! The moment, she exited the Museum knew God had a purpose for her life. She had an important triumph story based on survival trials as a teenager and childhood memories wanted to live on. A story, based on recollections from Silk City. The story developed at the sidelines of a great historical city that also wrote her story. Just like a novel, the protagonist was the young Newcomer; Rose Marie, against the fearless antagonist *Silk City; Paterson, New Jersey.*

Now older and wiser, Rose Marie needed others to know how *"I never gave up and continued to press on."* She tried the very best, until finally won by the only possible means, with God's help! She wanted others to learn God was in control of everything, no matter what she saw, heard, or lived! Rose Marie's mission recognized good triumph tales brought back hope and goodness in people. The experiences, she lived as a teenager was a constant reminder goodness won over evil. Although, at times bad decisions and desperate despairs twisted her spirit and soul.

Overall, the Newcomer's personal story was worth future generations know and learn. Rose Marie overcame uncertainties, innocence, helplessness and experienced first hand cultural shock. Besides, she experienced language limitations, social and economic barriers. Finally, Rose Marie exited the Museum and thought, *"After so many years, I finally know my calling!"*

She recalled all started during the early fifties when Rose Marie was in God's plans from the beginning of times, came into the world. Even before, she was inside her mother's womb; God allowed Rose Marie's birth. She was not in the parents plans. Since, they had just lost a newborn child; Hernan, who only lived for two days. Then, came Rose Marie first breath of clean fresh air, when the *barrio* (neighborhood) midwife named *Doña (Mrs.) Rosanna*, placed the child in the mother's caring arms. Nora in a homemade cot, gave birth at a small town *Aguadilla*, at the northwest tip on the Enchanted Island, Puerto Rico.

The young child saw the sunlight for the first time at the beautiful coastline. She was the second child, among six siblings. The island was the home for Rose Marie, during her first thirteen happy years. Her world was around the island and nothing else existed. She felt good at the island and thought it was the beginning; the Alpha and Omega, the entire universe! She could not even conceive the idea to live in another place, but the island.

Culturally, the tropical island was a serene place where people knew each other by their first names. Islanders, smiley dried faces by the sun and hard worked handshakes were enough to believe them. The islanders' words were valued and respected more than written contracts. Islanders, had time to stop, chat with neighbors and friends on dusty side roads or beneath shaded palm trees. They smiled even to strangers as they walked by and greeted each other. Willingly, they played the favorite pastime, a hand of dominoes anytime, anywhere until sunset!

Also, during difficult times the islanders offered encouragement to families and friends, as they helped neighbors at the hurricane seasons. Customary, the region storms reached categories four or five without previous warnings, or *FEMA* to send relief. Islanders, relied on each other and family members during disasters times.

Finally, Rose Marie memories of a small wooden church on a hilltop overlooked the ocean during childhood serene era. Rose Marie closed her eyes and saw peaceful times spend outdoors at the Caribbean island, where she ran freely as a kid. The backyard was endless miles of blue water beaches surrounded by high tide waves, light sand and plenty of sun rays.

As a child, Rose Marie watched the father; Dominick, catch fish for supper as he allowed smaller fish to go back into the water. Other times, he took the conch out of the shells and cooked outdoors for the entire family.

Meanwhile, Rose Marie ran fearless barefoot, collected shells, rocks, and starfish, until the iron bell announced suppertime. Then, it all happened! She became thirteen...

"Keep me in the apple of your eye; hide me under the shadow of your wings." Psalm 17:8

●●●

Chapter 3

SO POPULAR THEN…

"Jesus Christ is the same yesterday, today, and forever." Hebrews 13:8

Rose Marie recalled at age thirteen was the most popular, well-liked girl in school at the island. She felt loved by many friends. School was a special tight social net, where she felt protected. It gave her the confidence and security needed during those crucial teenage years to boost the self-esteem. Rose Marie's mind lingered with a sense belonged to a special place!

The young girl participated in every school activities planned by teachers. Willingly, Rose Marie participated in a small theater performance; during her sixth grade class recital, dressed in green. She recited a poem for the graduate class, which brought tears to those who listened and received a stand ovation. From that moment on, she clearly, established the artistic reputation, which followed her around. Other times, Rose Marie eagerly performed different characters, from a fairy godmother to an angel, or spy. Also, she did the characterization of Virgin Mary, and other Biblical characters. The audiences, were made of school's classmates, family, and the local community enjoyed performances outside the schoolyard. Usually, right after lunch the school yard open space served as an amphitheater, if the weather allowed on sunny days.

The young girl's heart and soul went into every artistic participation regardless of lines memorized or hours it took prepare. It started when classmates and friends supported the short skits outside the schoolyard. First, it was a game, until teachers discovered the talent hidden in her normally quiet personality, which transformed and exploded under the trees shaded areas.

Afterwards, almost everyone waited for the next performance after lunch. The schoolyard big enough, held large crowds whom applauded and gave standing ovation. Among, wonderful faithful friends were Mary Jeannette; her best friend; almost her shadow, Junior, Daniel, Glenda, Isabel, Ana Miriam, and Grisiada. Eventually, all friends stayed in the island except Grisiada, whom left to the Bronx, to seek a better tomorrow.

Meanwhile, among the audience were the beloved mother, older sister Jeanette, and sweet proud Taina grandmother. They came to see performances specially church plays.

On the other hand, Dominick did not believe in such trivial nonsense. Nevertheless, Dominick claimed, *"it was not proper for a man to waste time to see daughter's performances."* Furthermore, was unacceptable for his daughter involvement in the artistic world. According, to Dominick's train thoughts, was misused of time and unnecessary acting skills went nowhere. Dominick associated acting career with prostitution, which ended in low vain life undesirable activities. They were no exceptions according to Dominick; girls could only be nurses, secretaries, seamstress, beauticians, clerks, waitress, especially homemakers, but never an artist, which led nowhere. According to him, acting was plain foolishness that led straight to hell.

On the other hand, Rose Marie ignored Dominick's ways, since teachers at school promoted the artistic activities. One thing, Rose Marie was sure drama abilities helped her gain social status and popularity among peers. The acting went on for long time. If there was school activity, Rose Marie was there and acted out some character.

She went to schools at towns around the area gave the very best performances. Sometimes, came back with trophies, plus gained popularity and recognition. Rose Marie recalled *"the best epoch of my entire life."* She closed eyes and imaged the songs, dances or performance of the typical soap operas popular entertainment at the times. Rose Marie admired an actress named *Martha Romero;* a very beautiful and popular, who worked in movies, television, soap operas, plus radio shows. Such remarkable combinations, talent and beauty inspired many young girls to follow her example. Rose Marie was not the exemption. She loved the actress sweet tone voice during soap operas called "novellas." Many times, the young girl daydream was her daughter and worked by her side. Instead, she found immediate consolation as fan number one. Rose Marie remembered,

"Those were the best days of my life truly happy when everything was pink and I felt in the clouds!"

On the other hand, education was very important to the parents. They did not want their children to go through life without an education, like they had to endeared. Dominick, the only boy among five sisters, didn't go to school during sugar cane season, but instead worked the fields. He knew what hard work meant at the early age of seven.

Instead, Dominick forced by the father worked the sugar canes fields. They worked twelve long hard hours from six in the morning, until six at night. They took black coffee and a few pieces of butter-bread, while worked the long hot days. During sugar cane season, called "*zafra,*" the son worked instead of school, considered a luxury Dominick's parent could never afford.

Dominick helped his family that lived below poverty level. After much insistence from school authorities, Dominick went back to school until the eighth grade. During the 1940's, an eighth grade rigorous quality education was equivalent to high school or higher education. Rich kids, were able to continue with their education education.

Meanwhile, eighth grade gave an edge to Rose Marie's father whom wrote and read well Spanish, as he became best in math. He was part of proud graduate class of May 1942, rural school eighth grade.

Schooling for most poor folks was out of the question, even though the father had a unique opportunity to further his education. Virtuous in math, the school authorities offered him a scholarship to further his studies to become a math teacher.

Instead, Dominick chose to help his father and went straight to the sugar cane fields. He felt responsible, since he was the only male among four sisters in the family. Poor, father dreams put on hold forever...a lifetime. Though, he eventually put his math skills to work at the Lord's service, and became the church's treasurer for many years followed by a clean impeccable slate.

Ironically in 1942, while the dad emerged from the sugar canes, on the other side of the world in Europe's continent, Hitler immersed against the Allies in the Second World War. During this period in history, a young girl Anne Frank and family hid from the Nazis atrocity. They secretly hid on an attic third floor building in Amsterdam, with a very small window that looked to the outside world.

Young Anne kept a diary in a black and white marbled notebook. Eventually, Anne led the world know the misery and pain the family suffered while hidden. She wrote the first dairy entry exactly June 12, 1942.

Coincidentally, it occurred the same month and eleven days after Dominick's biggest day of his life. The other side of the world; the Island, Dominick's celebration of accomplishments, culminated with the graduation.

However, on the other side of hemisphere, ended sadly when the young girl's dreams began the downfall for the brave family. Meanwhile, Anne struggled to survive and put a fierce fight during two long years in the attic. Finally, the German soldiers found the family in the attic. Hitler killed all, except Anne's father, the sole survivor. What amazed Rose

Marie after all Anne Frank endured, still she believed in the goodness of humanity!

Exceptionally, Dominick after graduation became a soldier and a proud Veteran of the Second World War. In 1945, he fought against the oppressive forces and helped end the war where Anne Frank and the family were victims.

On the other hand, Rose Marie's mother was not so lucky in her younger years. She was a victim of social and economic circumstances of the epoch. The mother never went to school since was not permitted under any circumstances. The island's educational laws were not strongly enforced and most girls did not attend school.

Even though, the written law explicitly indicated, *"Children both sexes, school ages, must attend school."* The lack of responsible school authorities, and disrespect towards females were the sentiment shared among increase number of rural schools. It made almost impossible the enforcement of educational laws. It was secondary importance for poverty-stricken rural schools to foresee if girls went to school. Children abandoned to their luck by school incompetent authorities and irresponsible ignorant parents prevented females schooling during those harsh times.

Unfortunately, the mother was among those unlucky females. *"The woman's place was in the kitchen,"* folks constantly reminded Nora. Until, Nora finally believed the anti-woman philosophy. She grew up and became a good wife. Nora, being the oldest daughter, served the father and brothers. She had plenty practice, until one day became a good house keeper, a good wife, and then a good mother.

Therefore, Nora married at a very young age and became exactly what society and family expected from her: a good homemaker, a wife and an excellent mother.

"The mother's place is in the kitchen taking care of the family," Nora was brainwashed for many years. Eventually, all Nora's children grew up. There was no longer a necessity take to school. Then, and only then, Nora was "allowed" to go to work and helped the father. However, the process took long years to come about.

"The Lord is good to all; he has compassion on all he has made."Psalm 145:9

●●●

Chapter 4

GRANDMA'S LEGEND

"He leads me in the path of righteousness for His name's sake." Psalm 23:13

At the island, Rose Marie visited grandma Aleja, during gentle lazy days. Grandma made her feel loved and welcomed. Rose Marie followed grandma and watched her scratch the earth with a sow, until she found sweet potatoes for dinner. Every Sunday, the grandmother made sure Rose Marie went to church to learn the Holy Scriptures. Rose Marie learned moral and religious values on God, family, and the Precious Island inspired by grandmother's love. The gentle grandmother was a soft hymn bonded heritage and family values, made a big difference in Rose Marie's life. She remembered accounts recollected from grandmother Aleja ancestral heritage, endured from the beginning of times in the Puerto Rican history, until it ended with hostile wars that diminished the Indian culture.

Then, the Spaniards invaded and conquered the island. Many unfair accounts, vicious treatments to the Indian villagers were retold by Taino ancestral. The Indian Tainos fought for survival, beyond their humble control. The daily events around the simple life of the Indian Tainos enriched customs and traditions in the island. The the Indian Taino civilization legends were retold by grandmother.

The grandmother's house was an old broken-down wooden house a familiar place close to Rose Marie's heart. The grandmother walked from place to place or used a bicycle the only available transportation in the house. Grandmother; a thin sweet Christian woman, raised five children, while the husband was in and out relationships, a common trend for most male islanders during the epoch.

During the Depression Era, grandma Aleja, courageous enough brought the kids up, as best she could, regardless of personal and economic conditions worked the sugarcane fields to support the family.

Mostly, Rose Marie admired how never gave up nonetheless on matter how life treated, Aleja. She was a determined woman proved strong as an ox. In the fields, she picked sugar canes and loaded into trucks for long hours. Other times, she sold black coffee for two or three pennies a cup in the sugarcane fields helped by the daughter Lillian that carried the containers. Days, began early at six o'clock in the mornings, until six late afternoons. Then, the crew had thirty minutes to eat a piece of buttered bread and plenty of water.

Strong values and strict upbringings shaped grandma's beliefs, which guided her personal life. As well others, fortunate to have crossed her pathway.

Grandmother Aleja, always took time to teach the Bible. The grandchildren all went to Sunday Bible School. In addition, Aleja cherished stories about the Indian heritage and shared with family and others in the neighborhood.

Since childhood, Aleja heard legends of the Indian Taino civilization from her grandmother's side. Legends trapped in the past, reminisced ready for future generations learn and treasure throughout the years. Indians inhabited the island many centuries ago, known as, *"Tainos."* (Ta-ee-nos) Grandmother proud of the heritage did not waste time to teach the proper pronunciation of the Indian words. Aleja explained Taino were the last Indian civilization before Spain invasion conquered the island. Spain established the first governor Juan Ponce de Leon, an experience relentless soldier, came determined to conquer the island. The Spanish conquerors brought forceful work imposition to the Indians. In addition, enforced the language and the brutal Indians conversion to Catholic religion, food, home constructions, and customs. Drastic changes brought unique distinctive consequences of the rapid extinction of native Indians from long work hours and sun exposure without food or water. Also, the exuberant inhumane treatments gave Indians opium, instead of food in the fields.

Afterwards, African slaves were brought to the sugarcane fields to work, after the Indians extermination. Ultimately, grandmother's words stayed in Rose Marie's mind, *"be proud of the three mixtures in our culture: Indian, African, and Spaniard, made a unique Puerto Rican race!"*

Silk City

Proud Aleja, taught Rose Marie the distinctive characteristics from Indian culture commonly found in many people in the island. Indian features were noticeable by the remarkably visible high cheekbones, dark silky black straight hair, and distinguished beauty mark at the lower back or leg. These distinctive features identified Indian bloodline "Taino" in the islanders. Clearly, Rose Marie enjoyed the legend when grandma repeated her favorite Indian story. The family gathered around and listened carefully safeguarded each treasured word in their hearts about the extinguished Indian culture. Aleja took a deep breath in a trance without interruption began to speak:

"All started when the Indians inhabited the island many moons ago. The legend appeared with the native tropical flower five petals bright red, long pollen stigma called, "Amapola." (A-ma-po-la) The native Indians called Taino, direct descends from the Arawak's (A-ra-waks) Indians, first invaded the islands. The Amapola flowers were in each tropical island after an extraordinary event. The Tainos came down in canoes from Venezuela coast in South America brought the rare flower among their few belongings. They reached tip of the large Antilles in the Caribbean. The first blossom noticed in Tropical Island called, Borique, (Bo-ri-qen) was in a quiet village known as the Yucayeque, (Yu-ca-ye-ke) near the peaceful ocean.

At the village lived a young man, the only nephew of an old "cacique," (ka-si-kee) chief of the Indians called Guarionex. (Gwa-ri-o-nx) Everyone knew from the moment born; the nephew would become the next cacique. *"One day, he would be leader of its people chosen by ancestors,"* insisted the cacique Therefore, the villagers always regarded him with out most respect differently from all the other villagers.

The *"Bohique,"* (bo-hi-qe) spiritual guide, served as priest, medicine man, and elder told ancestral stories to the young cacique. The young cacique was the only bloodline direct descent of many caciques hundreds of generations ago. The custom was the first son born from cacique's sister, would become the leader.

Guarionex, the tired old cacique had many nephews, many sons, but only one sister left. The young chief Marionex, should occupy the larger square hut built in the middle Yucayeque, symbol of leadership as tradition demanded. Soon, he would fulfill his destiny.

In occasions, the rule brought resentment among many old caciques' sons. Only the spiritual leader, could retell story learned many moons ago. Ancestors decided how to choose their leader. All went into the next life, but left custom well alive among their people. Each generation selected only the first son of the cacique's sister. Ancestors wanted to make sure the next cacique had direct bloodline from ancestral caciques. The Bohique explained it was customary the caciques had many wives. In return, Taino men could have many wives too, including the cacique's wife. Custom passed from generation to generation without questioned and villagers accepted the sacred ritual. Young cacique Marionex, privileged with the highest honor

[37]

bestowed on him. Then, he became twelve years old and sent to a special expedition. Guarionex still ruler of its people sent him away with the special request.

The quest began with customary ceremony. The pursuit helped proof worthily manhood and measured his strength. It evidenced nature's harmony with the chosen one. His strength and power measured by the days he took to return. The uncle requested a rare flower never seen before by villagers.

For many moons, Marionex went away into the deep forest. He searched up and down riverbanks, behind waterfalls, and top mountains summits. He needed a unique flower, sign of strength and prosperity for the villagers. Then, the people would have good crops. In addition, the gods of the sun and water would give plenty water for the "conucos," planting area. The conucos were the areas women along daughters planted yucca for the casaba, corn and herbs needed for survival. Only then, would be lasting peace for the villages.

Finally, Marionex found a flower caught his attention. He never saw such magnificence wild specimen. Marionex amazed by its beauty called the flower, "Amapola" just like the love one back home. The five soft pedals reminded her peaceful and innocent smile. Just as the young leader cut the stem, he slipped down the cliff cut his thumb with the sharp ax. The stained blood turned pedals bright red. "What a beautiful red color," he thought. It made such contrast against the yellow pollen seeds that reflected the sun. "It looked quite enchantingly *different,"* he thought.

However, by the time he arrived at the village, had lost too much blood and became very weak.

The medicine man summoned quickly to the hut danced around the young cacique for days. The medicine man used special songs learned from the elders and secretive handpicked herbs from ancestral times. Nevertheless, nothing helped. He lost too much blood and was too late! The villagers wept for many nights. After all, the young cacique only hope was surely dying. Nevertheless, before he died the custom was to choose a wife. All the girls in the village wanted to be the wife of the dying cacique. After all, it was the highest privilege become the cacique's wife. Marionex chose the most beautiful girl in village. It was dear "Amapola." Then, they placed a large golden necklace that identified him as the leader. The bohique and old cacique performed a quick ceremony. After, he gave the rare red flower to his bride. The dying cacique gathered strength and spoke to villagers for the very last time.

He recognized his reign would soon end. It only lasted a few days. However, he warned, "The next cacique must bare beautiful flower Amapola sign in body and soul. Only the one with the mark of rare flower could be chief."

The bohique and uncle promised in mid Yucayeque to lookout for the rare symbol. Guarionex told elders and villagers of the nephew-dying wish. Last words must be obey, "Only the one with Amapola flower sign could rule his people," he insisted weakly. Those were his last words as he smiled weakly into the wife's arms. Gently, Marionex *was then positioned in sitting posture-clenched arms ready to go into the next life. Then, he was laid to rest. The wife drank quietly the potion and became sleepy. She joined him gently into the next life journey, the valley of no return. She would sacrifice her life just to be call, "cacique's wife," and wake up at the next life, beside her love one.*

Everyone sad for days, mourned inside the village boundaries. They accepted quietly god's way. Nevertheless, villagers never forgot words "look for Amapola sign."

Then, time passed and villagers were unhappy. They wanted a new cacique guided them to rule the people with justice and hope. Most of all, the villagers needed protection from carnivorous enemies neighbor tribes the "Caribs." (Ka-ribs) The Caribs took every opportunity attacked peaceful village, while the men fought to protect the village.

Meanwhile, the medicine man, assured villagers was just a matter of time. He insisted, "Soon, a new leader would be born with the Amapola flower, as spoken before." Bohique demanded patience while he waited for the five petal flower sign. On the other hand, old Guarionex demanded a nephew from the only sister's direct bloodline. For nine months people waited impatiently.

Time of uncertainties, went by while the cacique grew older and weaker. Everyone anticipated moment the new cacique would arrive and guide villagers against enemies.

At last, the time came. Everyone gathered around cacique's hut. They stood quietly in the middle large square plaza used for special occasions in the Yucayeque. All, wanted silently witness birth of the newborn leader. Inside, the large square's hut, the medicine man helped the sister who screamed louder and louder as the hours passed.

Finally, it happened. The newborn cacique was midst of village. There was a long silent moment. Only squelch owls and birds sounds were heard in the distance. Suddenly, the medicine man began to scream! Everyone looked at each other confused. The spiritual leader medicine man screamed louder and louder. Indeed, it was a scream of horror mixed with surprise! Something never seemed before interrupted the peaceful village. The medicine man could not believe his eyes. The gods sent a, "girl" instead of a "boy." It was a cacica, (ka-si-ka) girl instead of a cacique (ka-si-kay) boy. For centuries, had been a boy, but instead gods sent a precious little girl. Everyone, amazed the moon and sun gods sent villagers hope through little cacica girl. It never happened before.

The medicine man shook head and thought about ancestral stories. Slowly, he came out the hut. Bewildered, he told villagers new leader was a girl! Villagers whispered to each other puzzled. The old cacique came slowly out, too. Everyone hushed and knelt. "She shows on her back sign of the rare flower Amapola! She will be our leader in twelve years," he announced. Then, he raised the new cacique girl towards the stars. Villagers remained kneel. Everyone looked surprised at splendor birthmark. Surely, she bared the symbol of the flower beauty mark. Thus, the little girl was his only direct blood relative left.

Time, quickly passed by. The girl grew beautiful, strong, and wiser, recognized by villagers as the next leader. She liked long walks by conucos grounds women worked and taught daughters planting skills. The Taino women worked quietly in fields planted vegetables and fruits necessary for survival, while the men protected villages. Everywhere, she walked beautiful flowers grew. Villagers called her, "Amapola" on behalf of the beauty spot on her back. She was the only woman Taina to become leader of her people. She changed custom for the next cacique's generations to choose first-born son or daughter to become chief instead of nephew. She guided their destiny to prosperous time and recognized as one of the most peaceful leaders of her times. Eventually, villagers loved and felt deepest respect towards first woman cacica. During her reign, Tainos mostly lived in tranquility with their carnivorous neighbors. Ultimately, Amapola was killed defending her people against the Spaniard's invasion.

People visited the island, all four corners and could see the beautiful red flowers everywhere. It was a reminder of the beautiful Taina named Amapola, in Borinquen, nowadays the Island of Puerto Rico. Islanders recognized Taino Indian blood features in the high cheekbones, buck teeth, straight black hair, and beauty mark in the back or legs evidenced of the legacy Indian lineage.

(Indian Tainos' replica daily activities, Aguadilla, PR!)

Flowers used on women hair was a vivid testimony long ago lived first woman who became chief of native Taino Indians. Nowadays, it represents native national flower symbol of island's pride."

Lastly, grandmother took a deep breath. Proudly, she picked the most beautiful red flower placed carefully on her long natural shiny black hair. Aleja made sure the native traditional flower was on the hair's right side, taught by her great-great grandmother. She assured all Indian bonds remained stronger than ever before, were never forgotten from generations to generations.

Back into reality, Rose Marie recognized only the

grace of God kept her alive pushed by sweet childhood memories when grandmother picked up the pieces. Finally, time took its effects. Soon, Rose Marie forgot days in the schoolyard. Days started to fade away into fog morning. Vague lost feelings, turned into emptiness a reason to prepare for the trip. Shadow clouds yield filtered dim light into better days ahead. She promised friends never to forget. Sadly, farewell tears and laughter exchanged and good thoughts accompanied her sorrowful soul through the journey, to the voyage of no return. She promised to write, but somehow never had time or lost simply desires. Distance, life indifference combined with time, washed away promises, lost and forgotten like a bad dream.

Rose Marie had a chance for a fresh start with new friends at the Promised Land of milk and honey. After all, it was contagious the excitement to, "*Nueva Yol,*" that is, New York. Many, people called the new nation land of opportunity. She heard was the land of equality and righteousness, where hopes and dreams walked hand to hand. *"Oh, a new opportunity for acting among lots of new friends!"* With God's help, Rose Marie desired the artistic performances continued at the new city. Rose Marie thrilled about her new destiny at the far away land. Her thick white heavy glasses popular sixties frames fogged with pure anticipation. She fixed the glasses and looked at the magazines piles on the end tables in the bedroom. Rose Marie entertained the idea of one day would return as a famous Hollywood star. It was the trend for artist to have a star on the Hollywood Boulevard. The information came from the magazines, received as payments instead of money, while she babysat for the next-door neighbors. Contented with the magazines as pay, she fantasized with fame and fortune, and also decorated room with movie stars posters, envy of the village.

Finally, the day came. Rose Marie left with a faded small luggage grandmother gave for the few belongings. She looked back at the island for the last time. Skies full with brighter and shiny stars than ever, said good-bye. Skies clearly peaceful full moon, shined like never before. She would never again see so many stars huddled together for many years to come. Eventually, the beautiful sky sparkled with many stars laid hidden away for a very long time.

Heartbeats pounded loudly in the head, until it ached, but the young girl ignored the negative feelings ventured into the new life. Soon, friends left behind were small gray shadows, tunneled quickly out of mind, danced forgetfulness dance, became part of the past. Rose Marie could not remember all their names; just faded sun burned smile faces said. *"Good bye my friend."* She murmured back, *"Good bye."*

"Giving thanks to the Father who has qualified us to be partakers of the inheritance of the Saints in the light." Colossians 1:12

● ● ●

Chapter 5

SILK CITY HISTORICAL BACKGROUND

"Moreover, when God gives any man wealth and possessions, and enables him to enjoy them, to accept his lots and be happy in his work this is a gift of God." Ecclesiastes 5:19

Silk City people mostly lived without knowledge how illustrious city's name endured special timeless historical place. History acknowledged Silk City took specific paths throughout different perspective: culturally, socially, and economically. Treasured historic details described the outstanding individuals identified specifically as big achievers in the complex community. Three important reasons deducted by history itself that should be present: Silk influenced directly city's economic growth. Then, the composition of many hardworking immigrants and the very important inventions generated historical richness and renounce name for the grand city.

Silk City occupied by manufacture old brick cracked musty buildings cradled the Industrial Revolution. One of the most important men responsible for Silk City's development was Alexander Hamilton, who appears on the fifty dollar currency bills. He helped greatly city's expansion by his visionary dream used the waterfalls located in the midst of Paterson. Alexander Hamilton noticed potent commanding natural beauty site when he once stopped to rest and picnic near the falls.

Rumors claimed in one occasion, while Alexander convoy with George Washington, accompanied by Marquis Lafayette, a French military leader; fought next to General Washington's soldiers, Alexander stopped to admire breathless the area. Then, overwhelmed by the enormous beauty powerful force produced by the waterfalls remained in Alexander's mind.

In 1790, Hamilton held the highest governmental office position entrusted as the Secretary Treasury of United States. In 1791, the city established a group of investor's manufacturer textiles goods supported by Alexander Hamilton's vision used electricity power obtained by water force from the falls. Thus, investors attracted by the first city with own energy source.

Hamilton organized investors known as, "Society Useful Manufacturers" used raw materials, textiles, dyes, and silk fabrics secured independence for the industrious city. By 1870s, nearly fifty percent of silk throughout United States prepared in Paterson, therefore acquired famous nickname, *"Silk City."* The city generated uniquely electricity plant built on the riverbanks at the Passaic River surrounded by natures unpredictable beautiful waterfalls 77-foot high.

In 1831, Paterson was officially incorporate as a city. A name gave tribute and honored to William Paterson born in 1745. He was nonnative from Paterson, born in Ireland. In 1747, the Paterson family immigrated to Princeton, New Jersey. William Paterson helped organization of New Jersey's battalion forces during Revolutionary War, supported General George Washington.

It was a well-deserved tribute to thousands Irish immigrants' contributions in the city! Hooray! Nowadays, the electrical plant stands upright testimonial historical value from the flourished past.

Throughout, the lifetime William Paterson had great accomplishments worth mentioned. Among contributions, valued mostly were his personal merits: William Paterson was one of fifty-five delegates represented New Jersey in the Constitutional Convention, which drew document for the Constitution of United States.

In addition, he was an outstanding leader, lawyer, and Attorney General. William Paterson represented New Jersey, as a State Senator and later became Governor.

Also, William Paterson accepted prestigious position as an Associate Justice Judge at highest Federal Court. Furthermore, William Paterson called, "father of United States Senate," for administrative skills consolidated the United States first Senate.

Additionally, he updated New Jersey laws that replaced obsolete British laws. Definitely, such powerful industrial city deserved such powerful name! Moreover, William Paterson reinforced strongly Alexander Hamilton's economic strategy visualization for Silk City.

Alexander builder of Silk City's dreams and financial progress produced electricity from the Great Falls, advanced city adjacent areas economy and eventually the country. Also, there is a prestigious college with his name, nearby.

Nowadays, in remembrance a delightful Hamilton's bronze statue overlooks vigilant the waterfalls and guards the vision economic potential as a reminder of those who dared to dream. The statue faces the powerful Great Falls as a tribute and honor of this great man's vision. It was a tribute to the prosperity extraordinary vision for the city and country!

The visionary dream became very important to Hamilton's legacy and to the city of Paterson. Eventually, his vision flourished into the first prosperous producer of silk textile city moved by its own electricity.

As progress came, other outstanding important developments enriched Silk City. Historic economic contributions made people stopped and looked twice at Paterson achievements.

The city's rapid economic growth expanded nationwide. Among, the city's contributions were the first locomotive built self- propelled vehicle used by railroads pulling different mercantile goods and later used for passengers.

The locomotive built in Paterson, placed Paterson in historical books. According to public records on October 6, 1837, the train ran successfully first route from Paterson to Jersey City, then to New Brunswick, back into Paterson. In 1865, a Paterson man named Dan forth Cooke, built steam locomotive called Erie Mogul 254 displayed at the side entrance at Paterson Historic Museum.

[52]

Furthermore, John Holland, an American inventor from Passaic County, built the first small submarine equipped with gasoline for surface and electric underwater motor. Successfully in 1879, Holland submerged the first submarine built into Passaic River used dual propulsion system, again made history for both city and nation.

Hundreds newcomers, tourists, and residents enjoyed first-hand documents, photos, exhibitions evidenced historic times at the new home of Paterson Museum, on Market Street, the Historical district site.

The historic museum constructed strategically nearby the famous waterfalls, where it all first began. The Museum displayed the iron locomotives, planes replicas, and the first submarines as part of past glories.

In addition, another huge bronze statue located at a nearby park on Cianci Street, called the attention to Rose Marie. It had beautiful trees and flowers to enhance the area with the Great Falls nearby. The enormous statue seen from all angles belonged to one of the greatest comedian of all times that enriched the city,s history and all America. It belonged to Lou Costello, a native from Paterson, New Jersey!

The Lou Costello Memorial Park honor the man that gave so much to Paterson and therefore to all Americans! It gave tribute to the actor and comedian who made the country laughed with his innocent mischievous honest to goodness sense of humor even through were very difficult times.

Lou Costello

Hooray goes to Lou Costello's immortal words:
"Who's on first, what on second, I don't know who on third..." baseball sketch from his 1945 film.

Rose Marie thought how George Washington, Marquis Lafayette, and Alexander Hamilton walked and admired the same paths she loved. Probably, they stepped on the same stones, just as many others in Paterson, and left a lifetime footsteps while they enjoyed magnificence natures spectacular flaunt!

Frequently, many admired freely the majestic waterfalls, which cheered and amused everyone in sight. How splendorous God was! All over the country and adjacent areas, many came and witnessed the powerful breathtaking waterfalls full to the maximum capacity of water. Contrary, during dried drought seasons, waterfalls manifest minuscule detailed the bottom rocks formations could be seen, while the small streams ran freely.

Even under extreme cold temperatures, Rose Marie watched waterfalls small streams as it broke free from the inescapable frozen destiny low temperatures. Each spectacular site, created dramatic impressive scenes worthy of all Americans cherished and enjoyed.

"Listen to council and receive instruction, that you may be wise." Proverbs 19:10

●●●

Chapter 6

THE ARRIVAL TO SILK CITY

"In the morning, oh lord, you hear my voice: in the morning I lay my requests before you and wait in expectation." Psalms 5; 3

Cold breeze chilled the city when the Newcomer arrived quietly at sunrise new beginnings. On the other side, foggy smoke gushed from tall pipes, while the industrial city welcomed the new Latina girl to town.

Rose Marie's watery eyes, made it difficult to see beyond the immediate horizon. Countless tall smoke pipes splashed abruptly into the environment full of black spout and orange flames. The enormous rundown factories antique brick buildings, gave the city a frighten appearance. Enormous, buildings and similar houses embellished sidewalk streets. Unfamiliar siren sounds from fire trucks, plus ambulances rushed ruthless into the streets that already had an unbearable congestion from the everyday traffic.

Rose Marie's heart hesitated for a moment, but soon spun away in ecstasy as she thought of the future. Her humble docile heart embraced quickly happiness. After all, was the, *"in thing,"* to live in

New York! The most popular girl in school had moved to the congested city. She fantasized and felt would be better chance to fulfilled her dreams hopefully to come out of poverty, which held the family down.

It was the father's idea to take family so far away. One day he said, *"We are going to New York."* It brought such state of confusion, when she heard news, more like a command, rather than request, from the authoritarian father figure. She kept self-respect and safe face and looked at the move as something positive. She felt torn away, but never thought it would result in harsh damage.

Father waited at the Bronx, New York, for his family, with the mother in-law Aleja, whom managed to move a month before, with three older sons to an apartment. Six months later, Dominick left the mother's in-law house and went from a fast growing urban city the Bronx, in his opinion, to a slower paced city in the neighbor State, New Jersey.

Many jobs advertisement were placed everywhere as an invitation to come into Paterson, "Silk City," Signs seem all the way up to Tennessee's roads, advertised the fast growing industrial town, *"Silk City needy of workers."*

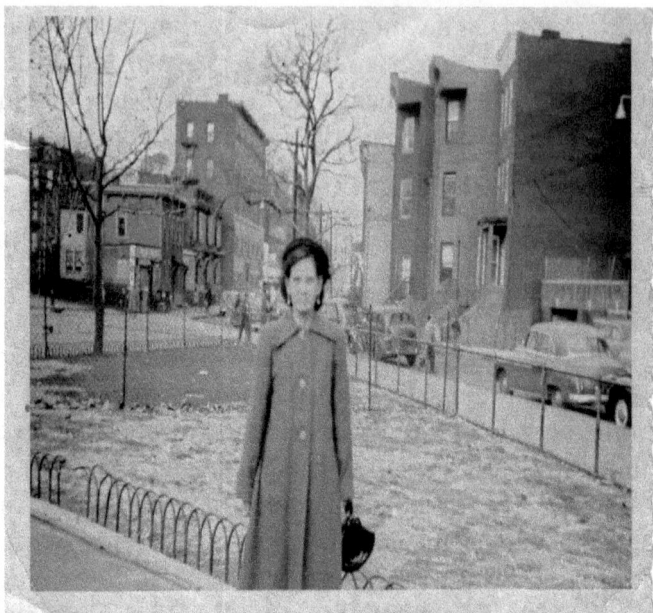

(Grandma Aleja when she lived in the Bronx)

The city well known by the industrial reputation welcomed good workers and increased opportunities to immigrants for an overall better life. The father optimistic said, *"We are going to make it in Silk City. There are abundance of jobs for hard workers like me."*

Nevertheless, it was not such an easy task to get a good job, but Dominick trusted the Lord with all his heart. He was confident with an eighth grade education diploma and an honorable Veteran discharged from the United States Army, would land him a good paying job. In addition, Dominick picked up few words in the language while he served the army. Still, Spanish features and his heavy accent made the process more difficult than expected.

Mostly, Dominick held back by the inability to explain his veteran's background abilities with limited communication skills besides the intimidation. Still, Dominick's language skills although remained inadequate for a long time, helped him through the ordeal to find a job.

Therefore, Dominick took the first unsuitable job offered without hesitation. He had little knowledge, and information on damages caused by chemicals inhaled or skin exposure after prolonged periods of time. *"Eighty dollars weekly is consider a good salary during those times, even if meant, working long hours,"* he explained to Nora. It was quite a temptation for poverty family of eight, which began all over again, during hard times. *"It's just a job,"* Dominick insisted.

However, Dominick never stopped to think about harms, or long-term illness due to improper protection caused by prolonged chemical exposures. One day, Dominick was diagnosed, *"Your lungs would collapse from a rare type of cancer, because of constant chemical inhalation and will result in ultimate death."* During, his early sixties the company gave him an early retirement!

One day, an unforgivable thing upset the balance of the family. Something occurred unexpectedly that broke family's unique bond forever. The oldest sister Jeanette due to a combination of poor health and cold weather, was unexpectedly sent back to the island. Rose Marie and the rest of the family were taken by surprise! Jeanette developed chronic asthma attacks, since she could not take the bitterness cold weather.

"Maybe, it was best for oldest sister with an easy going sweet personality," Rose Marie insisted in her mind. *"She could not have taken the insensibility from others."* Eventually, Jeannette's spirits would have perished among city's ruins. *"God knows what to do, and does it well!"* The oldest sister Jeanette was sent with the loving grandmother who neither could take the bitter cold weather wanted to return. Grandma Aleja reassured parents Jeanette's well-being would be best for both, to return to the island's warm weather.

Meanwhile, the strong-headed woman taught Jeanette strong Christian family's values and customs based on Taino's Indian traditions. The grandmother encouraged and supported education that would shape the sister's life. Eventually, Jeanette entered the medical field and became a well-known doctor. She was a precious pearl for the family and first to study at the prestigious, *University of Puerto Rico.*

Still, it broke the Newcomer's heart when she left behind the oldest sister. At the time, Rose Marie could not understand why parents separated them. It was difficult breaking bonds and assimilated the atrocious pain. The unexpected separation caused more pain to an already aching heart. Both were inseparable and Rose Marie missed her sister for the longest time. She could not take the loneliness, which grew deeper as time passed.

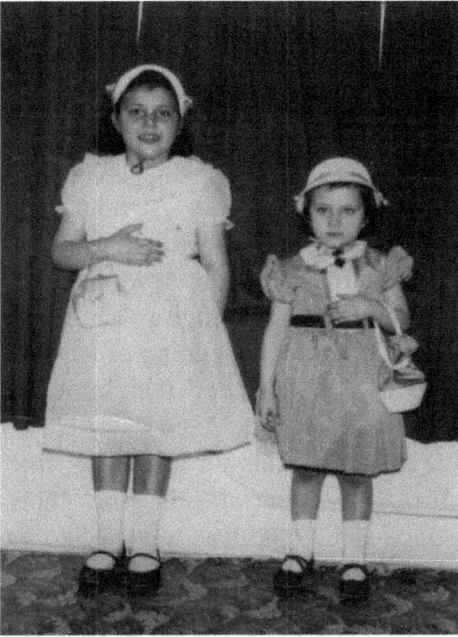

Rose Marie felt awkwardly out of place as resentment grew stronger towards the parents, which she blamed for her suffering. Rose Marie stared at pictures of them together during happier times.

At the beginning, when an airplane went by the beloved sister came to mind. Rose Marie ran desperately to the window until it was out of sight. She waved as thoughts of the sister on the plane brought relief and comfort to the throbbed heart. Meanwhile, Rose Marie insensitive parents casually mocked and joked about her silliness.

Indeed, how silly she was! The concept of distance between the island and city were yet unclear.

Often unconsciously, Rose Marie still wonders off after an airplane as she treasures the memories from the sister comes to mind.

After a few years, to make matters worse, the sister finished the nursing career and decided to married. She was moving away to Mexico, beginning a Doctoral studies together with her future husband. After, Rose Marie heard the news insisted on going to the wedding. Amazingly, she did not get permission to attend the wedding of her older sister.

This decision filled her with more resentment towards the parents. The excuses of lack of money, expensive plane tickets or absentee from school, were unbearable. Deep inside, she knew the real reason. Once again, she was treated like a child, and her feelings or opinions were not taken into consideration. Therefore, she was helpless with nothing to say, or do about the matter. Rose Marie did not forgive the parents for many years to come. At that time, their relationship deteriorated completely.

Years later, Jeanette and Rose Marie reunited physically when she came to visit Silk City, but as a Doctor, during a summer vacation. Although, physically they were separated spiritually their souls remained bonded as one. Just as today, even after Jeanette's death!

After a while, Rose Marie rebelled. The rebellion started slowly, as it emerged from deep inside. She was glad become the oldest and took full advantage. The girl felt powerfully important for a while, at home. She knew there must be a purpose for her life. She was born a leader at least, within the family. She took every advantage and opportunity to let the siblings know who was in control.

Her brothers, Hernan and Milton, and youngest sisters, Lillian and Ruth quickly learned who was in charged at home. Rose Marie became second in hierarchy, but for the siblings the oldest since physically Jeanette was not around to refute the position.

Mean hard glances, were all it took to claim space and territory between Lillian, Ruth, Hernan, and Milton. The boys, Hernan and Milton played cowboys and Indians, without bothered Rose Marie. While Lillian and Ruth played with dollies among themselves kept their distance.

Finally, the family settled in a small apartment, an area known downtown by *West Broadway*. It was a large, grayish, rundown five-floor apartment building. Spanish tenants from the island occupied mostly *"El Building,"* as it popularly called. Everyone helped accommodate each other as they watched many families move in and out, *"El Building."*

People from the building, made everyone felt welcome, as they smiled and pointed out a few details about the city. Quickly, they knew each other by their first names. They welcomed Newcomer's family and gave a helping hand to the father with the odd pieces of furniture from Salvation Army, a thrift shop a few blocks away. The *Building* was like back home, everyone spoke Spanish. Regardless, father insisted the family should keep to themselves.

The Newcomer surprised hardly anyone knew English, but there was certain relief not having the necessity of learning the new language right away.

Down a few streets, there was an Italian grocery store with Spanish products used back in the island. Eventually, the grocery was bought by a Puerto Rican, which lived at city for many years. He saved enough money by limited himself and made all sorts of sacrifices in order to buy the grocery business. Then, it was turned into the first *"bodega,"* the Spanish grocery store. It was the only Spanish grocery store located on upper Main Street.

The grocery store was a place where the Newcomer could get a five cents coke bottle and candies for pennies. The owner knew people's first names and considered customers his friends. Eventually, it became a landmark place for Puerto Rican.

In addition, the bodega was a daily focal meeting place that kept in touch with Island's news and traditions for the entire Latinos Newcomers. Men gathered and whistle flirting undesirable and annoying, *"piropos"* (intended sexual comments connotations) to Rose Marie, and other young women, which were ignored.

Afterwards as time went by, central key people helped the development and growth of what would become the strong Puerto Rican community.

Mostly, they came from a cozy place called, *"El Building,"* at West Broadway. Among tenants who helped transformed the city and opened doors for others ventured to show their best human qualities and qualifications.

Most important were the following worthy mentioned so their deeds would not go unnoticeable by the vast majority:

At the precious *building*, lived the first Spanish Municipal Judge Clerk Court Secretary, *Esteban Martinez*, who served well with dignity and compassion at the lower Court for many years until his well-deserved retirement.

Also, in the *building*, lived first department clothing Spanish Store owner. The store called, *"El Paraiso,"* like back home *Paradise*, located in Park Avenue, owned by *Julio Rivera*. Everyone went for first necessity articles and clothing items for the entire family. He always had a smile and served the Spanish community with pride and dignity.

In addition, the first Puerto Rican furniture store called *"La Luna,"* (The Moon) where quality furniture could be bought at comfortable prices with different payment methods accessible to the needy growing Hispanic community. The store owner was an outstanding community leader, greatest master ceremony, fundraiser, organizer, founder and First Honorable President of the Puerto Rican Parade in Paterson, who kept customs and traditions alive in Silk City. A special friend, loved and cherish, name *Domingo Deniza*. Hooray for such a valuable person among the community!

Followed by the tenant, *Rosa Velez* who eventually owned a family clothing store named, *"La Favorita,"* (The Favorite) on Main Street. Rosa Velez, was indeed the first bussiness pioneer woman to own a clothing store. She became very good friends with Rose Marie's parents and together went to the same Pentecostal Spanish church on Main Street under the leadership of beloved *Reverend Miguel Mena.*

In addition, were the young girls whom became teachers, social workers, secretaries and nurses such as, *Noemi* and *Sarah Torres,* daughters of well-intended religious loving, *"Suncha,"* Sister Suncha. She kept a watchful eye with all the girls in *"Building,"* under control away from temptation as she taught God's Word of love.

All lived in the same *building* at one time or another and gave their very best to the community. Today, an asphalt city parking lot replaced what was once well-known as the Puerto Rican *Building.* The structure once stood shaped many good Puerto Rican fellow citizens, helped produced the first city growing productive Hispanic community in Silk City.

"And we know that in all things God works for the good of those who love him, who have been called according to his purpose." Romans 8:2

●●●

Chapter 7

NEWCOMER'S STRUGGLES

Therefore do not be foolish, but understand what the Lord's will is. *Ephesians 5:17*

Consequently, at other side of the world Silk City, laid another torment mixed with satisfaction story. Perhaps something lost, but also gained, sometimes defeat and occasionally tasted victory. During late sixties, the teenage girl felt like an immigrant, an outsider in Silk City. Even though, Rose Marie was citizen by birthright since the territorial of the island belonged to the mainland, United States. In 1917, Jones Act granted mechanism for U.S. Congress gave citizenship to all islanders from Puerto Rico, which many still seem to ignore. Therefore, Silk City promoted great immigrants' inflow from everywhere. The city welcomed productivity and loyalty that were highly expected. Contrary, Newcomer became an outcast in the city when she could not generate either expectation. Constantly, Rose Marie struggled with confused identity wanted in her heart belong to the new country, but felt trapped in childhood memories from the island. Rose Marie felt betrayed by adults that ignored her true feelings. The girl found self-destructiveness induced by low self-esteem, an easier way out.

Dreadful years wasted as teenager in Silk City where suicidal thoughts came to mind as an easy way out. She thought about taking a few pills from the old rusty medicine cabinet or perhaps drinking a glass of *Clorox*. It seemed easy enough and would end her misery soon. There was nothing worth living for, at least she thought at the time. Nevertheless, the lack of courage prevented such deplorable act. The repulsive idea to burn in hell forever stopped the Newcomer right on the tracks. Simply, it was the hand of God's real purpose for her life. Then, Rose Marie remembered a man that sang and praised enthusiastically the Lord, from church week after week. Few weeks later, he hung from his bathroom's pipes overwhelmed with problems, too difficult to ventilate. Rose Marie overheard the father said, *"Surely, he would rot in hell, Lord Mercy."* He shook his head amazed by such cowardly act. *"God is the only one who has the right to give or take away life,"* he insisted.

Instantly her suicidal thoughts disappeared, as a foggy morning and never came back to haunt the young girl. Nevertheless, everything changed drastically and nothing was ever the same, as death was surely close by.

Rose Marie remembered the first glanced in the historic city, was at the splendor waterfalls amazingly natural elements caught her attention, and helped in difficult times. The Waterfalls contrasted sharply with intimidating tough streets on a crowded city. She could not believe such natural beauty surroundings flourished within city limits. The historical region helped conquered the unfamiliar culture during strenuous times.

Great Water Falls Park stretched for miles. Paterson unique attraction had the most beautiful waterfalls Crossover Bridge shortcut from one stretch of the park to the other side. The Newcomer walked over a long narrow bridge visited annually by hundreds of tourists. The bridge served as a turning focus point where many admired nature. The bridge exhilarated by the electrified water force overlooked impressively sixty-six feet down. The falls gushed deeply and rushed into the Passaic River, outlined by greenery plants, trees and superb rock formations.

She giggled about her thoughts, *"If God had to choose a place to live, and surely these waterfalls would be ideal residency."* Nature was only variance on her side that made less desirable circumstances a bit much bearable. Throughout, long periods of walks, Rose Marie found comfort and looked down the waterfalls, as it released enormous powerful amounts of water into the river. Sometimes, like a game, shadows tried indelibly to hide the sun an important element in her life. In the island, familiar strong sun rays kept Rose Marie, gently warm and safe.

At the waterfalls, she observed strong water thrust sparked the waterfalls as it hit rocks created a deep gash, like inevitable circumstances that cut deep into her heart. Rose Marie mesmerized by the natural waterfall magnificent sight during different season throughout the year. Often, she was hypnotized by the misty waterfall sounds bubbling water, splashed her face shocked the frighten girl back into reality.

A fragment in time, a peak fraction existence, time stood peacefully still in front of the intense waterfalls. Rose Marie found serenity ecstasy for a split second familiar similarities with greenery back home, as she licked her wet lips. It was a safe haven place for her throbbing heart during puberty years. The natural splendor was the only connected link, which brought hope to her miserable life. As result the, *"Latina Newcomer,"* labeled determinedly used essentials natural elements to sough her pain.

Nature brought peaceful harmony to the mind without allowing annihilation of her spirit. Rose Marie needed to escape from it all; just relax, watched God's creation beautiful waterfalls rushed down its natural path.

Rose Marie determined to succeed no matter what life brought on, as immigrants and grandmother Aleja! Eventually, Rose Marie had no other choice, but immersed into the new culture in Silk City.

The young girl captured by the new environment unintentionally created an odd sensation.

Furthermore, to make matters worse, the Latina girl with language inadequacy built a wall barrier supported by the hostile environment in school. To complete the uneven equation, cultural elements outlined the differences, the individual unacceptability and indifference towards her, against the atmosphere coldness. What a combination! Foul weather, combined with language barrier added by the total people's indifference, took a heavy toll.

Furthermore, inevitable inclement cold weather conditions made matters worse for Rose Marie. At the tropical Caribbean island, Rose Marie was accustomed to the hot sunny weather. The Newcomer brought warmth inside her tan skin, then plunged into the bitter coldness without proper warning or clothing. Most of all, Rose Marie had no psychological preparation that dealt with raw cold bitter weather.

Then, she faced the language limitations in the new city. At the beginning, Rose Marie had improper and limited language skills unable to communicate simple words and thoughts to others. Probably, others assumed she was dumb, plain stupid, with little social skills.

She never heard native speakers use the language so rapidly. It sounded differently from her sweet English teacher back in the island. The teacher had a soft broken-down accent and used the same book year after year. She used parrot-like repetitions with the verb to- be drilled day after day.

Rose Marie became accustomed to new meaningless routines in the new country. Irrelevant drilled conversations seldom used in real life situation. Those senseless repeated phrases useless or little contribution for a better quality life. Routines forced upon the Newcomer were boring and worked against her creativity free artistic ways.

She was sensitive, imaginative, and easily distracted to daydreaming and acted scenes with new words in her mind. Immediately she made the effort to learn more words to increase vocabulary to a much larger repertoire to communicate the simplest things.

Lastly, the human factor was worse than the bitter cold weather. Ironically, by this time, the weather started fell warmer than people around. She never was used to cold weather, but neither to the coldness found in people. Rose Marie faced strange behaviors difficult to comprehend. She tried to understand why she had to stand in the bus, while so many men sat. She tried to figure out why people pushed instead of waiting in line.

She tried to look the other way when someone stepped on her toes without saying, *"I'm sorry."* Coldness reflected perfectly the indifference upon the busy people up and down streets. Nobody, looked at each others eyes when they walked by, instead turned their faces away. There were too many cars and rude people in the streets. Rose Marie crossed streets, or cars quick or surely would have run her over. Where was the love for each other? Consequently, the emotional token took its course. Barren, reality hit Rose Marie hard, as she dealt with yet another problem, the first time she felt rejection. Loneliness was a huge problem and affected her the most. Therefore, she could not tolerate the indifference of people all around, so remained distant, lonely and felt an inadequate teenager. Rose Marie struggled to keep above all. She recognized would take time to turn indifference and attitudes around.

She had no one to turn for help or advice outside her folks. Parents, had also their personal demons to cope. Besides, it made matters more difficult being around her parents. Rose Marie unable to understand and satisfied parents expectations, became overwhelmed with her own problems. Constantly, the Latina girl blamed the lack of experience handling new emotions and such growing pains to the over protective old-fashioned parents. Rose Marie did her very best, but not enough to get over the rough hurdles without getting hurt. Her resentment grew stronger towards them.

Later on, she realized parents just reacted under difficult circumstances, personal language limitations themselves, which kept them isolated and clueless socially with limited language skills. Meanwhile, the gap between them became wider. They needed involvement and vision on the circumstances around her life. Instead, they were blind and deaf to the pain process not belonging to the city. Simply, Rose Marie homesick and lonely, drifted away from the family. Parents repeatedly told her, *"Don't worry; soon you will get used to all."* In reality, the Latina girl developed a deep depression.

From the most, popular girl back home, Rose Marie turned to be a complete stranger, *"unknown in the big city."* All dreams and hopes washed away.

She begged with tears and broken down voice, *"Please, father return me to the island,"* or *"give me your blessing to return back home."* However, going back was out of the question. It meant weakness and he was too proud to allow her return. It was not a choice left for her broken heart. Clearly, Rose Marie's opinions never sought, nor complains allow to be voiced. The father; the man of the house, made all decisions final for the family, and that... was that...

Then, she sought out help elsewhere. Rose Marie thought could count on people in school community for guidance and support. People in key positions she turned for help as: teachers, school counselors, guidance counselors, school authorities, which supposed to guide the younger generations. Unfortunately, no one ever question physical bruises or isolation. Instead, became silent participants of her apparent destiny.

Therefore, adults around became Rose Marie silent enemies, since they never lifted a finger to help figure things or where she belonged or make the process smoother. The adults around, Newcomer became evil instruments and despair when they decided to look the other way. Indeed, the new girl needed guidance, explanations on how things worked in the new city and school. The unwillingness to assist was unbearable, as she tried desperately to fit as a teenager. Limited cultural understanding was just the worst. To top it all, Rose Marie dressed out of style; not even a pair of jeans to her name. Women pants were completely out of norm, prohibited by church and the father.

Apparently, the conservative long skirts and long sleeves covered Rose Marie body and looked awkward. Then, there was the Spanish religious music and none English language spoken at home. The Puerto Rican customs and traditions, had different connotations, from rigid religion dogmas unacceptable in the city. The absent of the Caribbean foods, different holidays celebrations, as the Three Wisemen, instead of Christmas added to her isolation. While, snow melted slowly away month after month, so did the Newcomer's hopes, spirit and dreams.

However, as time passed everything seem further away from her wholesome insignificant life. Tears ran softly then uncontrollable, like the waterfalls. Either way, the innocent girl's mind suffered turbulent shocked intolerance from it all. Why did girls wear makeup instead of being natural? Why did people laugh when she could not pronounce the words? She waited patiently in the sidelines for a change. Other times, desperately dealt with all strength to stop mocked situations. afterwards, she decided to follow the narrow lonely road seldom taken, full of disappointments and despair in the new big city. Deep inside, she knew one day would become the conqueror, instead of victim, victorious instead of a defeater. One day soon, God will give her the victory...

"Those who seek the Lord shall not lack any good thing." Psalm 34:10

●●●

Chapter 8

CULTURAL SHOCK

Blessed is everyone who fears the Lord, who walks his ways. Psalm 128:1

Rose Marie discovered the awareness of being Puerto Rican, while she lived in Silk City. She never thought of herself being *"Puerto Rican,"* just a normal young Christian girl from an island without labels. *"Born into a Spanish language culture,"* she repeated several times. *"We do not ask, or demand any culture in particular, it just happens,"* assured herself. To a thirteen-year-old a birthplace whereabouts was the lease bit important. One day, Rose Marie forcefully saw the brutal reality she was different because of the birth place.

Rose Marie impressed how the over-populated city played an important role in her new life. There was nothing worse than the feel of an unwanted stranger within the culture. Then, came what was commonly known as "cultural shock." Everything familiar, became wrong and out of place. Unfortunately, no matter what she did to please others the hostile environment was a constant reminder she did not belong there.

Dark lonely years the, "sixties," prejudice rampaged towards the girl. Obviously, indifference to her needs, combined with ignorance and intolerance of being plainly diverse. It was an era that made sure everyone knew what being different really meant.

Strong cultural ties, heritage, and Christianity were not easily broken and simply forgotten. Someone with a cruel sarcastic laughter once said, *"Oh, how nice, more Puerto Rican to Paterson,"* At the time, the young girl did not clearly understand the true cynical comment's intentions. Though, those immortalized words pounded hard in her heart and stayed in her mind for a very long time.

At first, Rose Marie was optimistic ready to tackle the new environment. Thus, leaped into the process of acculturation, which began the moment she stepped into the city without warning completely unprepared. She was shocked by the language and its culture. Rose Marie tried learn through television and radio. Rose Marie listened to *"Uncle Bruce,"* on a popular radio music hit show. It was her favorite program, but the music was too fast beat and words meant absolutely nothing. In addition, Rose Marie turned the radio, or the television off in fear, just before the father came from work, since music or noise easily irritated him. She coped and looked out the window, as people walked the streets and imitated their dress codes, but nothing seemed to work.

Slowly, Rose Marie gave up then mocked and ridicule was devoured by lonesomeness. Her spirit almost broken into tiny pieces home sick, she longed for the sister and friends back in the island.

Since, there wasn't any one available to talk, she decided a drastic way out. She locked herself in her bedroom with an old radio, for days. The young girl, only came out to eat, or used the bathroom without speaking to anyone. Quickly, food became a relief, as she over ate and easily gained weight. She ate until it made her sick. Every opportunity, Rose Marie blamed the parents for taking her away from the childhood friends and family. The resentment grew stronger and boiled inside, ready to explode.

She remembered how the idea to start over again first came from the locals at the small town of Aguadilla influenced by politics. The small town was surrounded by the silhouettes chains of mountains called, *Cordillera Central.* (Central Mountain Chains) that stretched east to west, the place where it all started.

The widespread propaganda came from *Luis Muñoz Marin*; a gifted bilingual politician, lived in the mainland and was familiar with American lifestyle. Luis Muñoz Marin was the son of the leader, *Luis Muñoz Rivera;* a philosopher, and writer. The father, Luis Muñoz Rivera, was the first elected Residence Commissioner to Washington, DC. Under the father's leadership, came the creation of Popular Democratic Party, in Puerto Rico, later known as the ELA. Then, Luis Munoz Marin followed the father's political footsteps. During the Governor's campaign, Luis Munoz Marin used a new strategy with transcendental results. The direct contact with the working class had never been done, before. Marin visited the humble hard workers agricultural class located on the island centered chain mountainous coffee plantation towns.

The coffee fields' workers lived in small houses provided by the plantation owners. Luis Munoz Marin drank coffee in their homes, a popular beverage of the region and the second main product, produced by the land. He presented his political ideals under the slogan *"Pan Tierra y Libertad."* (Bread, land, and liberty)

Afterward, Marin assured voters his true intentions boosted island's economy with stronger industries for sugar and coffee. He insisted on tourism as the key that would create stronger ties with the mainland and eventually increase the export on coffee beans. All this unique plan, boosted islanders' confidence, as he visited such remote regions. Two years before, in 1946, the island had a Governor appointed by President Harry Truman, first Governor of the island, *Jesus T. Piñiero*. It marked the Island's history with *Jesus T. Piñiero,* the first native citizen held the highest office after Spain reign.

Nevertheless in 1948, Luis Munoz Marin became the first elected Governor by the people, not appointed by the United States. People trusted the candidate for Governor, who quickly gained support. Luis Munoz Marin gained their self-reliance and respect and resulted in the island-wide election winner. Therefore, he became the first elected Governor under the Popular Democratic Party.

Until 1948, newly Governor Luis Munoz Marin elected by an overwhelmed majority encouraged islanders to cross-ocean to friendlier prosperous land in the United States. The country was bonded by citizenship and strong economic ties, which he assured united both countries. Rural islanders knew through *Operation Bootstrap Economical Program*, promised to build the island with better tomorrows helped by United States. The newly elected Governor assured islanders during frequent radio addresses, strong democracy bonded the island and the country. The islanders bombarded with eye-catching advertisements, of once in a lifetime opportunity in the new country were the best place to search for job opportunities to find the American dream; guaranteed entitle by citizenship rights. Despite good intentions, island's economy took time to boost and balanced itself with the new Governor, while the rest of the world recuperated from the Great Depression.

Every day, soft whispers to leave island became louder and louder, while government television announcements, political radio speeches, newspapers, and magazines articles boosted intensive public opinions. On the far away horizon, laid Silk City, prosperous on the other side of the world, called like soft mermaids whispers looked for the golden pot. Many islanders went to the mainland. Islanders could not ignore during the precarious World Depression deeply affected the island's economy.

Besides, the atrocious hurricanes, one after the other, had taken its toll destroyed houses, crops, livestock and even life. Food was scarce even with seven dollar a month Food Stamp program presented by newly elected Governor to ease island's economy. In addition, the Governor established popular "Shoes," program. It provided a pair of shoes for each school age child. Usually, kids walked barefoot to schools. It was the first time most children from the island wore shoes to school. Children suffered diseases due to malnutrition, unprotected feet from parasites and germs from lack of shoes. Mostly, victims were innocent children inhumanly suffered parasites through open wound feet cuts made them very ill, and in some cases resulted in death. It was the first time, the needy island had Food Stamps and a Shoe Program. The islanders, took the Governor's words very seriously embraced the new neighbor, the United States of America.

The thought to leave the island became an enticing idea hard to ignore. It had profound influence on most of the poor working class. Immigration started as a dominoes effect movement. One family member, followed another. It was an opportunity to have basic human necessities supplied to the family. Indeed, time to become a first class citizens, instead treated like a second-class citizens. The islanders had rights, proper shelter, food; clothing provided by good paying salary, education for children, and proper health care. Those promises not easily ignored linked directly to the country that represented democracy. After all, the islanders lived under the tyrant Spanish reign for too long. Finally, the citizens had the power to make own decisions and find richness in a country considered the World Potential.

Immediately the young girl's father, who served in Second World War, took advantage of the announcements. He knew basic English language and that was a plus. The father was among the first ones that left without looking back. He could not come across a decent paying job after he served as a soldier, no longer a farmer. Others, followed and immigrated to the new land and felt quickly into the dreamy mist. Although, many dreams turned into nightmares when forced to live in deplorable conditions among roaches, rats, and severe weather conditions. It was different from poverty already accustomed to very little. However, to live in sudden fast cold moving city unknown places with high expectations and unexpected outcomes were quite a different story.

Immigration flow quickly caught on. Citizens were lured by governmental authorities encouraged emigration to open boundaries to the new land, "streets of gold and honey." Perhaps in their minds, took words literally and saw kicking abundantly gold on the streets. The young girl's family felt right into the trap. The father never looked back and ordered the family to follow him. He left as soon as he had the money together for a plane ticket. He embarked at only available airline Pam–American, an eight-hour long dangerous frighten flight.

"I will not forget you. See, I have inscribed you on the palms of my hands."Isaiah 49; 1

●●●

Chapter 9

BACK AND FORTH...

"But the wisdom that comes from heaven is first of all pure; then peaceful, considerate, submissive, full of mercy and good fruit, impartial and sincere." James 3:17

Meanwhile, the young girl looked forward for the first freshman day in high school. Rose Marie liked school. It was a special social place, with many social possibilities to find new friends and advance in the her artistic presentations. Perhaps again, she would feel special like once back home. Before, it could occur, the mother walked the Newcomer up and down the streets in bare toes summer shoes in winter.

The mother needed to show the way about ten blocks from the apartment, with several turns and traffic lights. The Newcomer could go by herself to school, only after she learned the way. The younger brothers and sisters at elementary school needed more attention from the mother. Then, came the unforgettable school preparation rehearsal dreadfully began.

Rose Marie wanted to learn the way back and forth, as quickly as possible. Then, she would feel liberated from her mother. On the island, the young girl walked long distances by herself, approximately two miles, or perhaps more to get to school every day. She could walk to and from school with practically her eyes closed. Besides, Rose Marie walked long distances, from the mother's house to the grandmother's house. Her mind flew back for a few moments, spiritually into her grandmother's arms and listened to Indian's legends next to the oldest sister.

Now, at Silk City, the mother insisted Rose Marie was too young, furthermore it was dangerous to walk by herself. The entire time, mother upheld the terrifying idea her child would get lost or kidnap at the unfamiliar city. To make matters worst, without the knowledge of one word in English. Rose Marie did not mind the walks back and forth the streets: Van Houten, Ellison, Park Ave, Broadway, River, Straight, Market and so forth. Rose Marie learned the streets names with a Spanish intonation.

Both went up and down the streets stopped to admired fashionable stunning front window stores. "The Fair," known by their formal elegant superb gowns, on upper Main Street. On the side of town, "Lynn's' store average prices were well in the reach of most poor people located at Van Houten Street off Main Street. Paterson was famous for its fancy dazzling popular Quakerbush Department store, across from the famous Meyer Brothers and other renowned stores, side by side on Main Street. The crowds came from everywhere to shop in well-recognized beautiful downtown Paterson area. The famous stores made downtown streets come alive, with colorful new fashion and many adjacent towns came, also.

During the holidays, there were excitement to see the lighted fancy decorations on the streets, while shoppers huge crowds searched for holidays gifts. Mother and daughter took their time and looked in astonishment at stores never seen before in the island, especially during the holidays. They never entered or bought anything, but the mother sighed, while the daughter hoped someday each would have money to make a purchase.

Soon, they learned how many immigrants took advantage at the popular River Street thrift stores. River Street was famous for the many thrift stores side-by-side, able to buy everything possible according to their low income. Father also explained mostly everyone from church, took advantage at the funeral homes and bought formal suits and jackets for a couple of dollars found at the second hand stores. The suits used for special occasions on weddings, or preaching, were worn first by a dead person!

Still, they walked together, which was quality time for both. They shared old stories from back home. Mother and daughter laughed about the new experiences in the city continued quickly up and down the streets.

Excited, Rose Marie learned and listened carefully to mother's instruction. They decided to set markers to know exactly where they were without fear to get lost. Then, she saw for the first time what should be the next World Wonder, the Great Paterson Waterfalls!

Silk City

Rose Marie walked back and forth when she first encountered the Great Falls. She discovered the waterfall overwhelmed water overlooked a wooden bridge. It became Rose Marie's favorite place for peace and solitude, where she found freedom. Rose Marie meditated on God's Scriptures, while the water flowed like vivid waters in her heart.

At last, they arrived to school opposite side of town. The tall intimidating brown, musty building seemed huge; at least at the time. It reminded her of movies with dragons, dungeons, and monsters that thrilled the imagination. She felt so small standing in front of the large brick stone building double doors chained and padlocked.

Little, did Rose Marie know, soon the place would become like a cell prison, for her free loving soul. Subsequently, it would be the place where the girl's free spirit die slowly, surely a spiritual death. Why was there so much security? Most people she knew back home were good, simple, harmless, most trustworthy free.

She wondered why the school doors remained chain and locked. Schools back home were open spaces where the sunshine breeze caressed the children. The spirit of freedom roared in and out the windows. The doors, floors and broken-down wooden windows squeaked loudly as children ran in and out the rooms.

The schools far away, were nothing like the huge dark buildings in the city. The schools back home were small cozy with simple chalkboards several wooden seats and benches. The fragile structures needed rebuilding every time a hurricane hit the island. She shook her head tried to keep those thoughts from the past out of her mind. She concentrated in the present situation as chills and pure excitement took control once again.

Two large flagpoles stood in front defiantly, waved each a huge flag. She never saw a flag with so many stars. Back on the island, the flag displayed one large star was customary to be fully displayed in municipalities and government buildings, too. The iron flagpoles made such harsh noises of metal clanged against the pole, regardless of rain.

It seemed each flag wanted to blow away to escape from the high post. One flag belonged to the newly acquired nation, the other represented the school's spirit. Years later, she heard rumors a cemetery was near the school grounds. The sight frightened a bit, but enthusiasm drew tears back. For a moment, she hesitated, but entrusted the future. Soon, she would walk through main entrance with an open mind and heart. She had never known places beyond open, flat, plain one-story spaces, back home. Years later, Rose Marie had the courage to look back and thought clearly, *"It was only a four-story brick building that impressed me so much."* A young girl's eyes saw with her heart instead of eyes.

Finally, she walked several times again back and forth assured the anxious mother knew the way. This went on; until the girl confidently could recognize markers set by the mother even with her eyes closed. Finally, was the last formal rehearsal.

They passed by the Good Will store, first marker. She recognized it immediately, since they bought several necessary articles at reasonable price for the family's budget. Among things, was a piglet cookie jar displayed on top of refrigerator without cookies for decorative purpose.

The pinkish pig jar resembled the large piglets back home except, it had a cute dress with a greenish bow. It cost the mother fifty cents, for the beautiful piglet ceramic cookie jar! Nowadays, sits, as a relic in mother's kitchen, remains a silent witness, reminder of those horrible times. Then, came Salvation Army Store, the second marker. The coat still had the heavy mothball odor. The coat picked up by her father, a size smaller. After all, he said, *"What do I know about clothes for girls?"*

According to the father was not a man's job. They were to be grateful, since each had a coat. The smelly coat tightly clenched the girl's body. It snapped tightly, burst at the seams, and almost popped open when she vigorously walked down the streets. Still, she felt lucky though the bitter cold air penetrated down the coat and settled inside her bones. She felt stripped down naked down the streets with little protection from the cold. Her nose felt like ice popsicles as she played with smoke curiously coming out of her mouth.

Winter coldness began quickly that year. Another typical mist January cold day penetrated the young girl's bone. Rose Marie's body felt an awkward awareness of the bitter coldness never felt before. Her mother assured, *"the weather would be fine, just takes time to get use to it."* The young Latina did not care for the abrupt changes in the weather. She thought, *"the bitter cold was not about to stop her."* Rose Marie noticed strong winds changed hit unmercifully her face.

Thus, she went exactly the way mother had shown. Now, Rose Marie was ready to tackle the future. Shockingly, a blizzard came few days later and registered eighteen inches or more record for that winter. Finally, rehearsal was over!

"How many are your works, oh Lord! With wisdom, you made them all; the earth is full of your creatures." Psalm 104:24

● ● ●

Chapter 10

SPECIAL CHURCH CLOTHES...

"For you did not receive a spirit that makes you a slave again to fear, but you received the spirit of sonship. And by him we cry, "Abba, Father."
Romans 8:15

The Newcomer began to focus on the first day of school. Rose Marie got up extremely early felt quite uneasy with hiccups. Newcomer's hands were sweaty a definitely nervous sign. The young girl took a deep breath in great need of oxygen. Usually, Rose Marie felt the oxygen from the heavy green trees back home.

This time, she decided to ignore the burn feelings inside the chest. She continued to prepare for first encounter with school and surely her new friends.

Rose Marie took out the very best garment to wear. After all, she wanted to make the best impression in the world. It meant to take out the only good pair of "Sunday shoes" brought from the island. The shoes were shiny black covered toes and open heels. "At least the toes were covered," she thought. There were neither stockings nor socks to protect the feet from cold.

Then, the young girl took out an item from the small cramped closet she shared with the sisters. It was the very best Sunday clothes. Soon, it would make the biggest impact possible among the new friends. She read somewhere in a magazine that the first impression really counted and it should be the best, since it lingered in people's minds.

Carefully, Rose Marie laid out the best-printed yellow flowery cotton summer skirt, and a short-sleeved plain yellow blouse with a small left pocket. Slowly, she put extra care on the finest special Sunday church clothes. She stood upright in the mirror to button the blouse's delicate pearly white buttons. She wore the clothes proudly and knew it was impeccable.

At first, the skirt clinched to the skin. She swirled and twirled around and around until she felt dizzy. The skirt formed waves of soft fabric ready to swirl away to an ecstasy flight to school. For a brief moment, she flew away in her imagination, full of anticipation.

The stream of consciousness traveled miles away to the Tropical Island. Rose Marie thought about the first time she worn the yellow skirt with the pretty blouse. Yellow, was definitively her lucky color. She saved penny after penny, until had enough money to buy the soft fabric. It took her a long time putting the money together. Sometimes, she baby-sat for three pennies an hour.

Other times, she created a clubhouse and charged a few pennies dues to enter the clubhouse. Somehow, she managed to put the money together, Rose Marie bought different colors fabrics and the mother; a superb tailor, stitched gracefully the clothes. She remembered back in the island the pretty dresses were center of conversations. Mostly, everyone admired the popular girl.

Every, Sunday after church, at the town's main square, with benches and fountain, in front of the big Spanish architectural church people gathered to talk and showed off their very best. Every Sunday, it was customary gather at the town, a custom brought by the Spaniards. The square constructed in middle of each towns came from the Indian villages.

The Indians used the squares for ceremonies and games called, *"areytos,"* (a-ray-tos) to celebrate good crops and victories against their enemies. After many years, it became the islanders' favorite place for bohemian activities and younger generations to meet.

Many bright colors cotton materials for the hot weather, fluffed around the town's square. Almost, like a parade the beautiful coy women admired by the young men watched carefully and winked their eyes, or blew kisses a signal of admiration.

The young bashful girls, stopped at the water fountain intentionally and glanced naive at the young men. Rose Marie recalled once walked around the square with the older sister to watch the young boys. Rose Marie had to remove the confetti from her hair quite annoyed as the girls giggled.

Then, she finally understood the purpose of the confetti. She remembered, how she silently with her eyes looked at the young boy who conquered her heart.

Those were times of self-discovery, soul searching and innocent sexual awareness under the strict values learned home and in church. Those days were far gone, never to return. Times, she will never forget, only repeated in Rose Marie's mind! It was time to go to school in her beautiful Sunday clothes! Finally, the most waited first school day came.

"The Lord will keep you from all harm-he will watch over your life; the Lord will watch over your coming and going both now and forevermore." Psalm 121:7

●●●

Chapter 11

SNOW...

"Since you are my rock and my fortress, for the sake of your name lead and guide me."
Psalm 31: 3

At last, Rose Marie was ready for school. Before, she entered the classroom, there was a requirement to register. Everything was perfect! Suddenly, snow started to fall. She remembered the first time snow came down, customary of the region.

The snow made everything seemed like it was another planet. It was beautifully tranquil, just like paradise. Endless snow fields seemed soft and gentle from the window.

At first, it looked like a site taken from heavenly vision. Until, cruel awoken by melted dirty marsh splashed fiercely down her coat. The Newcomer touched the snow and tasted taunt flakes for the first time. There was no other choice, but become use to the extreme weather.

Rose Marie knew the weather could not be change and was out of her control. At least, she could seek cover and protection to prevent the harmful effects. Rose Marie used the coat to kept from the cold. She kept warm inside her heart too, since good vibes thoughts never died.

Mostly, snow covered the ground by the time she left to school. It was the first time she walked in the snow. During that particular day, she did not want anything to bother. Then, she ignored the snow and continued the original plan to register at the most desirable high school.

It took more time than Rose Marie expected to get acquainted with snow. Indeed, more time to walk in snow with her good shiny black Sunday shoes. There would be boots hopefully on father's next paycheck. First, he must pay rent, electrical and gas bills and then purchase groceries for the entire family of eight. The family could think about boots or other winter necessities after all the bills were paid. However, it took some time.

Everything was covered with snow. Suddenly, the Newcomer felt the toes dug inside the snow until they became numb. It was surely a dramatic cruel awaken call. To make matters worse, the father decided to take the young girl to school. Dominick the household head, had to sign the registration forms.

Meanwhile, Rose Marie felt down in the snow, but the father made jokes every time she came flat down. He reminded to practice, *"just try again, soon you would learn to walk in the snow."*

Father joked and comfort the young girl. Before long and many attempts, she stood up determined to walk in the snow.

The snow flurries on her hair, coat, toes, and legs made her feel stiff. To make matters worse, her fingers were completely numb without gloves.

Ten blocks seem endless, longer than ever. The more she walked, the further away it felt. The snow continued down fiercely hit her face without mercy. She could hardly breathe. Finally, they arrived to the last block.

"Humility and fear of the Lord bring wealth and honor and life." Proverbs 22:4

●●●

Chapter 12

THE SCHOOL ARRIVAL

*"Blessed is the man who perseveres under trial,
because when he has stood the test, he will receive
the crown of life that God has promised to those
who loves him." James 1:12*

Rose Marie astonished how snow turned the dark brown building almost white, an expression of superb architectural outline. The sun sharply reflected the snow and somewhat impaired her vision, but the father jerked Rose Marie's hand, to continue as fast as possible. Her heart beat so fast, it ached. Nervously, she cleaned snowflakes from the glasses and coat and swallowed her pride to continue the quest in the bitter cold. She needed to overcome the snow, since school, new friends, and the world waited with open frozen arms.

Upon, the arrival the father desperately rang the school bell and hit the double doors several times, at the same time rubbed the frozen hands. He spoke quickly in broken English and pointed to Rose Marie's personal documents.

Immediately, both gained access into the main entrance, which had secure padlocks. The doorkeeper; a janitor, listened while he closed the padlocked doors behind them. Inside, was much warmer, Rose Marie's glasses fogged and became instantly blind for a few seconds. The halls were extremely quiet, but occasionally they heard echoed sounds from far away. The school gave the impression of being deserted. The long spacious halls gave a cold Gothic sensation with the white marble stairs and walls. The Newcomer had never seen closely a marble wall before. She remembered similar structures in museum and mausoleum in the black and white movies back in the island. *"Where was everyone?"* She thought and touched the impressive white marble walls.

Then, Rose Marie caught a glimpse of an enormous theater. It had many colorful rows cushioned chairs and a huge red velvet curtain covered the wall. Rose Marie's heart pounded loudly at the place caught her attention. She never saw such a huge place inside a school before. Immediately, the girl felt connected.

Amazingly, she gazed inside breathless at the sight of many comfortable chairs for performances. There were straight rows red chairs, put together not seen, even in the wooden church, back home. The large stage caught her curiosity and thought of the rather small schoolyard space under the trees. It served as a rustic stage back home. Later, the Newcomer learned the "auditorium," was the place for assemblies and monthly live performances.

It was the perfect place for future performances already set in mind. Rose Marie wanted badly to be an actress. Surely, the right place for her dreams to come true. Briskly, the father shook her arm and brought back from dreamy dismay.

At the principal's office, papers were filed away after given a number. The two older women in the front office handled the registration forms in an automatic manner. Glances without real interest were exchange among themselves. They continued their work and took no particular curiosity to the new Latina Newcomer. The young girl felt warm and the face turned red. Rose Marie decided to remove the coat that still smelled like mothballs. The glasses clouded up and could not look straight into the principal's eyes, but felt him examined her from head to toes.

Rose Marie walked behind the principal guided through the quiet long hallways to the classrooms. The principal talked and pointed as if she understood each word. At the same time, her face red of embarrassment felt strange unable to understand the school process. She could not comprehend a word he said and felt uncomfortably awkward. She knew he spoke English; after all, it was the official language.

She tried to listen carefully to figure out the words. Maybe, she could recognize a word from own language to transfer in the mind. He spoke rapidly like spit bullets, despite the fact she was not a native speaker. There was no consideration, nor translation, or second thoughts. Everything seemed automatic and anomalous. Finally, her brain gave up and looked blank. Rose Marie followed without exchanged looks, almost distant and automatic.

Then, Rose Marie saw the father disappeared in front of her eyes. He left without goodbyes or a few words of encouragement. Rose Marie wanted to cry and run after him. She was terrified. For a moment, she stood alone in the middle of an unfamiliar cold marble hallway.

The Newcomer closed the eyes and asked God for help. She stood there like in a vacuum motionless similar to a trance. The girl was in the new environment, far away from home. Oh, how she wished to be back on the island cuddled in her grandma's arms!

"Have no fear of sudden disaster or of the ruin that overcomes the wicked, for the Lord will be your confidence and will keep your foot from being snared." Proverb 3:25-26

●●●

Chapter 13

BELL RANG...

*"The Lord is my rock and my fortress and my
deliverer." Psalm 18:2*

The principal brought Rose Marie right in front of
a classroom. He motioned to enter the room and then
left. Once inside the classroom, the Newcomer
would present the program card with different
classes to the teacher. The teacher then would choose
someone from the classroom, designated to help the
Newcomer to familiarize with school buildings and
find way around other classrooms.

All alone, Rose Marie was in front of the
classroom about to open the door, not knowing what
to expect. She did not have the slightest idea what
would happen next. She took a deep breath to ease
herself into the room. However, the bell rang as she
thought, "Saved by the *campana,* bell."

The bell rang loudly enough to be heard back
home. She wondered if her dad heard the stunning
bell. Back at the island, the teacher used a small
golden hand bell. The students recognized the soft
sound from all directions ran back to their rooms
quietly.

Subsequently, the new sound became louder and
louder until it finally subdued. Then, all hell broke
loose. Students came from all different directions
pushed, shoved, and shouted their way to the next

period on time within the four minutes allowed to move around. Some walked, others ran. She moved out of the way, but they were too quick and came from everywhere. They ran into hallways pushed and screamed as they slammed her body right into the wall, without looking back. She stood with her coat clenched tightly in her fist. Static from the cotton material lifted the skirt cringed to the body, as she desperately moved away.

Then, chaos! They all laughed, screamed and pointed continued down the corridor. Rose Marie felt miserable and nauseous. Some of the students, stopped to mock her, and whispered to each other, "the *Puerto Rican* new girl," pointed to the cotton flowery clothes. Everyone knew the Latina new girl in school with summer printed clothes in mid January, during the severe winter.

Between bells, the students always passed, pushed, slammed the lockers while they yelled to each other foul words. Every chance, they pointed and pushed the Newcomer who felt more an outsider. At first, she could not understand why they behaved so badly. Rose Marie sensitive tears flowed down quickly. They unmercifully made fun of the Newcomer, and all she wanted to die from embarrassment.

The Newcomer all alone in a super crowded school felt lost in the huge four-story building. She could not believe was among such an unfriendly cold crowd. There was not one face in the hallways she recognized with a friendly smile. Maybe, the girls with the teased-up sprayed hair that wore tight pants and heavy sweaters would offer friendship, or a glance of sympathy towards the Newcomer.

Rose Marie did not dare to look directly at their overdone make-up faces with curiosity. She feared they would take the opportunity to mock. Regardless, the students in the corridors never forgot the summer yellow clothes worn in mid-winter during the first school day. Most students, wore wool sweaters and tight jeans with high heel boots. Rose Marie looked for Spanish classmates for support, but all were unfriendly, too.

Throughout the last year of high school, mocking, giggles and laughter continued. Instead, went straight through gates of hell, as she referred regretfully to the school. High school years took away the best years of her life, until she finally caught on.

High school years should be greatest experiences for anyone filled with happiness of those unforgettable years. Instead, the Latina girl lived the worst times of sorrow and despair that destroyed her self-esteem. She blamed the unknown school system community where unfamiliar faces were not always welcome.

Simply, she did not belong because of the low tolerance with her skin color, sex, language, culture, and mostly religious belief. She reached a point, prayed God and asked to die, while contemplated the idea to jump down the Paterson Falls to finish all! Nevertheless, God had other plans for Rose Marie, what he begins will end regardless of the circumstances! Three years passed and still Rose Marie made only a few friends.

Finally, senior year was here. Graduation was a silent goal that pushed forward no matter what came her way. Rose Marie looked forward to get out of school. She continued as an outcast with the loud rock in roll music, tight clothes, high heels and indifferent to students in the hallways.

The Latina remained unwelcome and unpopular in the new school culture. She did not mingle in the hallways and tried to disappear quickly into the classroom safety. Rose Marie refused to stop and talk about trivial things mostly from fear. The gentle Latina girl never recovered from the first impression, but came with such high hopes and high spirit, but never recuperated from the first official chaos.

Rose Marie's ego was badly damaged almost destroyed so thoughts on being young, innocent, and pure taught as a child in the island did not make much sense On the contrary, these thoughts were not good enough as a teenager in a big city. A place, the strongest took advantage against weakest personal traits. It was an odd sensations being unwanted an experienced never felt before in the island. Bullies' waited in the sidelines prompt to take advantage fed from her weakness, uncommon in the island. What would friends back home think if they only knew her trials?

"All things work together for good to those who love God, to those who are called according to His purpose." Romans 8:2

● ● ●

Chapter 14

THREE WASTED YEARS

"Though war may rise against me, in this I will be confident." Psalm 27:3

Indeed, Rose Marie recalled how those three years slowly passed. She remembered immediately felt unaccepted and unwelcome when first arrived to the mix neighborhood high school. She lived at Franklin Street, a dead-end, where kids gathered in small groups. Instead, Rose Marie never came to mingle in the street, terrified with the idea to see someone from school.

She went through three unbearable years and shed many tears, until there was nothing left. Three years, she felt less than anyone else, with self-esteem broken into pieces. Rose Marie dignity and innocence were stripped away in such violent atmosphere by bullies. At the classroom, she felt completely ignored. Although, at the hallways was all a different story. Everyone knew her, but for wrong reasons.

Each period, between classes Rose Marie was either ignored or humiliated, since did not speak the language properly. Also, she wore differently the hair or did not follow the dress codes according to students' standards.

Instead, she became the laughing stock of the bullies in school. Bullies took every opportunity to attack the girl, just for fun, without anyone to stop them or intervene on her behalf.

Rose Marie remained unable to get the proper help since the parents were busy at work with their personal problems and never knew or understood her reality. The Newcomer remembered a particular day when she begged the mother not to send to school. The Latina girl felt drained by the hallway scenes and the unbearable cold weather. So, she took a chance with her mom. Furthermore, Rose Marie knew mother would let her stay home unless was a good reason for illness.

Instinctively, she walked slowly down the streets to figure ways to stay out of school. She was determined not to go to school that day and thought out a plan. After a moment, it started to roll. She walked into a building halfway to school to warm up. Eventually, she was thrown out by the proprietor, who was irritable, impatient with a low tolerance towards Latinos Newcomers.

Afterwards, she waited just enough time for school bells to ring. Then, instead decided to return home with a good excuse. She needed time on her side. The young girl was too late for school. *"I lost track of time when I warmed up in the building, before I entered school,"* Rose Marie calmly explained. She figured by then, it was too late to enter school, mom surely would let her stay home.

The reality, she knew it was late to enter school, without classmates humiliation and a good explanation to the Attendance Dean. She returned home in deep distress. *"Maybe, mother would let me stay home just this once,"* she thought. Instead, mother made her go right back immediately. Even, if she was extremely late and quite embarrassed, no excuses were accepted. She knew better than to lie ever again to her mother.

There were no recollection how the day after that transpired. Rose Marie must have been in automatic mode felt miserable. That night, Dominick punished her by not allowed to go to the church social event. The mother did not interfere with the fit punishment. The girl never tried to stay home again. Education was on the top list despite feelings and personal emotions were at the bottom list. No one cared, what she thought.

Ironically, during those three years the huge auditorium became a safe haven refuge for her soul. It was the perfect place to hide. Usually, she escaped to the auditorium from the ugly world around her. Only there, she felt safe as back home in the island. Then, Rose Marie quietly sneaked carefully in the darkness to the second level removed the chains that blocked the entrance. She hid without apprehensions, day after day. What a relief!

Finally, Rose Marie bonded with the special place of her dreams. Rose Marie buried her fears in the auditorium. Eventually, it brought out the beast we all have quietly inside. Transported by the huge stage she pretended to play out the lines in her head and gave the best performance. The girl heard the applause, until they became ephemeral. The agitating thoughts constantly drifted her thoughts away.

Thus, she daydreamed in and out all day long, until the heart desired and nobody interfered. She did homework, as plays came to mind.

The enormous rows of chairs protected the Latina girl from being caught as she escaped to the auditorium almost every day from the bullies. The secret peaceful place, Rose Marie learned to be alone with her thoughts. The Newcomer would run to the second floor at the dark auditorium blocked with rope chains. Rose Marie removed them carefully and hid all the way in the back.

Forcefully, she saw everyone in two categories: acquaintances or unfriendly. She casually knew a few classmates with common native language. Conversations were simply hello, class business, homework, and good-byes. She remained distracted, quiet, humble, isolated, and self-conscious of her limitations. The once popular girl died the same day she entered the cold marble building. Rose Marie remained lonelier than ever throughout three long years. She hid in dark shadow auditorium and felt invisible.

Though, she fought with all her strength not to end isolated and lonely. She had been around good people most of her life, but Rose Marie became afraid being humiliated and hurt most of time. She could not believe for the first time, *"afraid to meet new people it could not be true! Oh God!"* She felt abandoned.

Slowly, Rose Marie became a complete stranger to family, and friends. She decided keep to herself, as means of protection. In time, self-imposed solitude slowly carved deep scars into the heart. She became angry and distant to those around. Most times, she cried quietly herself to sleep. Apparently, she had a very high price to pay as the *"Newcomer, recién llegada."*

Rose Marie became distant and withdrawn... Afterwards, Rose Marie recognized God provided the auditorium, so her spirit would not die from so much pain.

Eventually, she went into a special English class separated from the main stream. Under the circumstances, she did poorly in the effort to learn English. The Special English class provided help to Spanish students who came from other countries not speaking the language. Students from the special class acted pleasant and smiled. Occasionally they said "hello" when they crossed paths in hallways, but were afraid of the bullies and fought their own survival battles.

They also belonged to an unwanted group placed behind barriers created by their native language and cultural differences. The Hispanic, "Latinos" became a subgroup, stained, and labeled by total indifference. There was intolerance for their inability to speak the language and communicate thoughts and feelings. They were demanded to learn the language quickly by teachers that became impatient and felt helpless themselves.

The group suffered daily personal humiliation. The right to be yourself or just plain different was stripped away. The humiliation to be from another culture was an everyday event. The idea not to know English and have an accent were conversation topics in the cafeteria followed by cruel mocking. Thanks for Henry Kissinger, Secretary of State, to President Richard Nixon. He made it acceptable and enjoyable, even popular to have foreign accent.

Meanwhile, cafeteria territory was off limits hostile environment, and Rose Marie made sure to keep away. Rose Marie, unknowingly, ignored the dress codes and trends used inside or outside school was ridicule and mocked. The cruelties were punishment enough for three long years. Rose Marie was guilty of cultural ignorance, language limitations, unaware of trends, and unfashionable with the clothing.

Daydreaming about childhood memories school years back in Puerto Rico, helped the young girl get through those rough three years. What kept Rose Marie going? She kept sanity through strong ties to island bonded by childhood memories. Rose Marie could fly away using the imagination.

She closed eyes and saw ocean waves and dusty roads led unto small villages back home next to grandma Aleja. Aguadilla, a small town on the hilltop overlooked ocean not far away from her memories. Some days she felt more sensitive and tolerant than others, it all depended on her state of mind each day.

Rose Marie continued daydreaming as means of escape from her miserable reality. She remembered the first kiss behind the principal's office back on the island. It was a simple cheek kiss, which made her blushed when she felt the wet lips. She ran back to classroom and hid from the kid.

The reenactment of the kiss made her happy, as she touched her lips. He was the first boy she had really liked. He knew Rose Marie was his girl. He would go by the house on a beautiful stallion. Then, he stopped right in front showing off his horsemanship skills. Through smiles and watchful eyes, she could tell, was his girl. The wink, the smile, the kiss…

Every opportunity in the classroom Rose Marie would escape, into own secret world. Overall, in there she felt beautiful easing the pain while struggled with her sexuality, inner conflicts, above all, language issues. In the classroom, she continued daydreaming, until one day a teacher threw an eraser to the head and brought back to cruel reality, while others laughed.

In school, Rose Marie noticed a Latino boy called, *"Frank."* She melted away every time saw him in the hallway. However, the boy was very popular and never took real noticed. He never spoke a word with the Newcomer. During, different periods of the day Rose Marie saw him down the hallways towards the lockers, close by. The newcomer shocked when she realized he signed the yearbook a year later, *"to a real cute girl, whom he will never forget, best of luck, with love, Frank."*

The Yearbook, called *"Senior Mirror' 68,"* was a treasured so much loved and looked over, from time to time. Occasionally, Rose Marie opened the yearbook and wondered about her innocent platonic love and classmates, hoping by now, they also made it after all. In addition, Rose Marie had tender memories of the gym class. When spring came around the gym teacher took advantage those few beautiful days to hold outside physical activities.

The newcomer ran fast, as if was back home. Afterwards, she cooled down in the sun yearned so long. Rose Marie sat on the stairways near the field, where a popular well-known girl smiled and sat next to her sun bathing. Every time, the teacher took advantage of the day, they would sit together after the run just to sun bathe. Rose Marie would close her eyes to let the sun caress and bathe the body recuperated strength which felt back home. Then, it became a habit.

Every opportunity, she sat and absorbed quietly the sun rays, strangely so did the girl without crossing words. Strangely, they never talked to each other just sat in the bleachers or at the stairway. Surprisingly, she signed the yearbook, _"wishing good luck to fellow sunbather and hopscotch partner."_ It was game played well as a kid back home. Those few moments gave the Newcomer a break from bullies remarks meant a great deal. Yet, she never gave up, and hung tight until the end.

"Commit your ways to the Lord, trust also in him and He shall bring it to pass." Psalm 37: 6

●●●

Chapter 14

THE TEACHER THAT CARED...

"He himself is our peace." Ephesians 2:14

Among the people, remembered with good vibes was the Spanish teacher. She was a soft-spoken woman who showed kindness with a smile. The teacher from time to time was the only one who spoke in the native language, when necessary to help her out from a tight spot. She had a slight accent, which made her sound even more beautiful when spoke Spanish. Her words were music to the newcomer's ears.

The teacher smiled gently when passed by the hallways. Sometimes, the teacher walked with Rose Marie to her class. She was like an angel send by God to protect the young girl. Those occasions were heavenly; bullies stayed away, and evil hurt remarks stopped.

Occasionally, the teacher would give her a pass to the bathroom or library during study period, in which the girl would take advantage and escaped right into the auditorium.

Other times, the gentle teacher would give permission to sit in the Spanish classroom, during lunch or study periods. Sometimes, the young girl felt so uncomfortable would look for any excuse to visit the teacher's room. She would stay for the period and listen to the Spanish class, as she closed her eyes to release the stress of the day.

As a result, the bullies tired to wait for her after school left home. Then, the newcomer would leave school by other exits or took a much longer way home to avoid confrontations. Every day, she maneuvered different exit doors or periods to leave as a survival skill against bullies. Meanwhile, the bullies waited impatiently to victimize the Newcomer after school. Soon, she learned to outsmart the bullies.

The Spanish teacher always treated her with the outermost respect and decency, such as many other teachers, but mostly were unaware of the real problem. On the other hand, the Spanish teacher kind, gentle, and soft-spoken became aware situation wanted to help the Newcomer. The teacher reported the students involved and eventually spoke to school authorities, which were in the lookout for the bullies, but were never caught in action.

The teacher never knew her interference reached the right places and eventually was a great help. The teacher helped the girl through those rough years indirectly eased the pain by just cared and gave support. Rose Marie stayed in her classroom without words or explanations made a big difference in the girl's life.

The teacher somehow knew she needed time to gain composure and re-organize thoughts before going out to the battlefield. *"Mrs. Lopez,"* always will have a special place in her heart.

Rose Marie wanted personally go back and visit the school to thank her, but it never happened.

The young newcomer struggled, but continued to put up a fight for survival. The inner voice told her something had to change. She knew the time had come. She needed to do something to stop the throbbing pains inside her heart during those terrible years.

However, she continued to hide at the auditorium every chance possible, other times in the bathroom, or at the teacher's room. Every day, was a new struggle. Every, possible way invented or redesigned was a way out, simply to escape from the bullies and survive… one day at a time!

"The Lord has done great things for us and we are glad. Psalm 12:9

●●●

Chapter 15

THE 1968 CLASS...

*"He who has begun a good work in you will
complete it until the day of Jesus Christ."*
Philippians 1:6

Summer finally came and another school year was
over. Rose Marie worked for the first time in a
nursery school sent by the summer school's work
program. Rose Marie took gladly the first job
offered through the summer program.

In the nursery school she could show freely the
little ones her love bottle up inside for a long time.
She enjoyed summer because of the weather and the
long walks in the Great Falls. The work enabled her
to buy basic necessities and stayed away from the
parent's hundred percent control. Work was a new
experience offered in the new country that she truly
liked.

At last, she began to fell useful and valuable. Rose
Marie loved to work with children where she could
laugh and giggle without fear of being mocked. The
children inspired the girl to continue in a new path
where she recognize a new call. It gave Rose Marie a
reason to ask God for new strength and more energy
to pursue future. It had been, after all a long summer
vacation. She had time to recover and rebuild
strength and power to push dreams forward.

Immediately, she used the paycheck for new glasses. She wanted to get rid of the thick heavy glasses, which made eyes looked bigger than really were. There was an immediate need to look for modern trendy style.

In addition, she got a slight haircut. She begged and finally got permission from the parents to get a haircut. The Pentecostal religion did not permit haircuts Somehow, she convinced the mother and then the father, until an inch came off. The nice haircut and fashionable glasses helped boost the self-esteem.

Finally, time came to return back to school for the Senior year! The opportunity to enjoy the last Senior year. During the long summer, she was full of hopes and energies. "One more year to go," she thought. Soon, she would be out of school and able to go back to the island next to the oldest sister and perhaps pursue an acting career.

Rose Marie wasted no time took drive lessons paid by the money saved during the summer. Money for a new car was also in her immediate plans. Soon, there would be less walk through the streets where the bullies followed and"hated" so much.

In addition, Rose Marie found the courage to go into the cafeteria. At first, she bought an ice cream sandwich worth ten cents, the money was saved for a car. At the beginning, she would not dare to buy food, even if she was hungry. Rose Marie brought a sandwich from home and sat in the cafeteria instead of hide out. She became friendlier with the Hispanic students. They treated her with kindness, respect, welcomed and actually relax.

First, they made small conversation about trivial things, but then attitudes changed and it was off to a good start.

Although, she regretted during the Senior year never experienced going out on a date, or to a dance. Rose Marie never heard about, *"Senior Prom Day,"* until her Cuban friends explained. Therefore, Rose Marie was not extremely bothered when no one asked for the Prom. Classmates, *Griselle*; now a respected and loved school principal, and *Mari;* her cousin, knew the ordeal with the bullies, became good friends.

The Cuban mother and aunt of *Griselle* and *Mari* insisted to make the Prom dress, just in case she wanted to go. Rose Marie admired the young cousins, which treated each other more like sisters. It was a relationship deeply admirable, *Mari* and *Griselle*, her very good Cuban friends!

The young girl entertained the idea to go to the Prom. Rose Marie daydreamed about the dance and fun, but in reality had two left feet and never learned how to dance. Besides, she knew Dominick, would never allow to go to such activity.

Meanwhile, the relationship with parents continued to be less tyrannical and oppressive. It was acceptable to visit the local *Pentecostal* church for spiritual guidance. The church located on Marshall Street, had the biggest Hispanic congregations under the leadership Pastor, *Miguel Mena*. The Reverend Miguel Mena was well-known and liked, an outspoken Pastor, leader in the Spanish community. Most people, from *"El Building"* attended the Hispanic Pentecostal church. Most all, looked for his guidance and help. Nowadays, the street carries the name Rev. Miguel Mena, well-deserved tribute for his contributions in the Hispanic community.

The newcomer, became good friends with his daughter Isis, and brothers. They saw each other in church, where it became a socializing place to meet new friends with the same Christian values and interest. Isis became best friend and confident. They enjoyed their times together even when she went to a different rivalry high schools.

Occasionally, there were opportunities for social supervised activities like weddings, birthdays and youth outings went Rose Marie accompanied by Isis and the Pastoral family. Nevertheless, there were no movies, nor television; called by the father the "devil's box," neither friends, shopping, sports or recreational activities allowed. Rose Marie never rode a bike. Once, she tried to ride a bike and felt down so hard, it was enough to stay away from bikes. Rose Marie was neither allowed to receive friends at home. She never had a social life. The self-confidence around boys started to emerge back in island, but became inadequate and underdeveloped for a long period in the city. However, the young girl, who entered school and longed for grandmother and sister, was not the same girl finally reached the Senior year!

"Those who shall wait on the Lord shall renew their strength; they shall mount up with wings like eagles." Isaiah 40:31

●●●

Chapter 16

TIME TO FIGHT BACK...

*"He shall call upon me, and I will answer him, I
will be with him in trouble."*
Psalm 91:15

The leader of the bullies had always looked for
opportunities to hassle Rose Marie, who did not fight
back for three long years. Sarcastically, during the
past years the bullies took every occasion to make
the Newcomer's life miserable. The leader made
sure the pressure was on to Rose Marie. Especially,
with verbal abuses tortured young girl and cried
afraid of the bullies.

The leader with a smirk smile on her face,
followed the Latina girl ever chance possible. The
cruel bully, made jokes about the nationality and
called her despicable names, "four eyes," and "spic."
The bully, constantly made remarks on her simple
clothing and reminded others about the inappropriate
summer garments worn during winter season. The
bully never missed an opportunity and made the
vulnerable Latina girl miserable in the hallways, in
classroom or outside school, when she followed her
half way home.

The leader with a group of students followed the
bully's lead in the corridors. Sometimes, it was an
angry group led by the bully, until they got tired or

in problems themselves by the school's deans. Sometimes, the intimidating group followed Rose Marie down the streets, until she disappeared into a building, took the elevator and pretended she lived there.

As a result, Rose Marie escaped home by different tactics. At times, she used different side exits from the school building. Other times, the girl took alternative routes home to survive the situation and confused the bully, who thought they figured out her behavioral and walking pattern. Sometimes, Rose Marie walked with the Cuban friends and stayed in the house until she made sure they were not around. Other times, she left earlier to avoid the leader; a girl, which hated her so much. All this maneuver, went on for three long miserable years.

The Senior year, the bully came back and thought things would be the same as past three years. However, little did the leader know the last year Rose Marie, came back tired of being a victim. Finally, came the day when she took control of her life. She decided to stop the isolation and suffer for so long. The change had to come not only from the outside, but also from within. It was time stop pain and misery ate her life too long. She knew the Senior year was the right time!

Two months, Rose Marie matured quickly saw things differently. Rose Marie felt different inside. She did not feel any longer, like a Newcomer. She decided an unusual approach from past years, when her thoughts and spirit were fix on negative experiences. Rose Marie knew sad events needed to forget, in order to turn her life around. She was tired of sucking up old regrets and frustrations, which led to isolation and despair. She wanted to look ahead, after all was once in a lifetime being a high school student.

She stayed focus on good vibes felt during summer. Then, one day it happened! For the first time, in a long time, Rose Marie felt in command of her life, once again. She remembered giggles and laughter energized her teenage spirit back home in the island. She wanted to come back with laughter and smiles as natural antidepressant. She was tired of tears lonely victim of the same circumstances day after day. Now, she wanted to be alert, alive, positive specially popular once more. The idea of college, began to grow quietly in her mind and helped push forward.

It was the first school day. Surprisingly, Rose Marie greeted everyone with a hug and kiss. She did everything in power to stay away from the girl that made her life depressed, stressful, and full of hatred. She did not want another class with same girl. Therefore, again. Rose Marie had a brilliant idea! She wanted to change the class schedule.

The Latina girl needed a different class to avoid cross path with the bully. She doubled check and made sure not to cross-corridor with the bully headed to the main office. She had been several times in the guidance and counselor's office, and requested college information, but to change a class would be the first. The girl used a work excuse, during afternoons and needed to leave earlier than the year before. In reality, knew the math class was the common link between them that ignited conflicts.

She did not want to take the same class as the girl, and avoided it all together. She could not take another year specially the Senior year, with such humiliation. Simply, Rose Marie was emotionally different, but still obviously feared the bully's loud dirty month and group attacks.

After proper changes from one office to another, Rose Marie remembered the moment when she entered the new math classroom and felt relieved. She careful went to the assigned room, after all did not want to look as a fool. The Latina girl looked around the students in the room. Then, it happened. She could not believe her eyes! Oh no! There was the bully with a smile again! Rose Marie became paralyzed and pale, as she walked slowly inside prayed God to help her.

For a brief moment, she panicked when realized once again had fallen straight into the bully's path. Surely, Rose Marie thought, "would be torture for one more year." Fate had handled her the wrong card, once again. She wanted to run out and screamed out of desperation, but she remembered the Acting class and held it together, as if nothing went through her mind. She acted as natural as possible. After all, no one knew about the schedule change. In the back, sat the big bully and smiled victoriously, as she walked by for another year victimize again.

Then, Rose Marie heard the squeaky, nasty voice customary repulsive remarks and called her the "S" despicable word. To top it all, her compulsive laughter broke clumsily invaded the classroom atmosphere thin line. Everyone, remained silent, waited for the next step. Something, immediately went inside deep the Latina soul like a bolt of electricity, more like a jolt of fire exploded in mid air. Rose Marie felt electrified, with thundered fired ready to ignite. A rocket fuel injection had finally ignited inside her, yet the sick fearful sensation to the stomach disappeared completely. The Latina girl's rage became explosively uncontrollable without thoughts she moved by instinct. Then, Rose Marie stood up and answered with the strongest strange voice the guts could produce.

Rose Marie followed with the strongest punch ever delivered into the bully's face. Explosive words continued to pour out of her mouth more like bullets in Spanish, others in English. For the first time, the young Latina followed with the continuous fist to the bully's body. This time, instead of being humiliated and embarrassed, she fought back with all her strength. She not only used a strong viciously voice tone, but grabbed the bully with all the bottled strength at the hair and throat. She did not let go for a long few seconds, which felt like an eternity, until satisfaction and enjoyment came with every moment of the bully's pain. She had finally released all the fight back power kept inside cramped for so many years. It was pay due time! Rose Marie enjoyed every bully's tear shed with a huge smile and satisfaction. The tables were finally turned.

Rose Marie looked straight into her eyes and returned a few spiteful phrases learned from the bully herself. *"Now,"* the Latina girl said in a rough voice. *"Don't you ever, I mean ever, dare to humiliate me in your life, again!"* The words fluently came out in well-spoken understandable English.

The teacher and some students intervened and Rose Marie stopped the pull to the bully's hair and let go throat, but not without taking a fistful strands of hair. Rose Marie did not realize strength, until she was pushed to the limits. The Latina girl finally responded to provocation, as she asked God to stop the bully forever.

For a bleak moment, she enjoyed triumph, an instant victory more than the standing ovation back in the island. There was rage in her eyes, since the bully never came close to bother her again. Everyone, knew Rose Marie finally stood up and defended herself.

The class bell rang, but this time had a different sound. Everything changed, Rose Marie walked out straight, looked at every one in defiance, but proudly took a deep breath. The next period both were at the principal's office. The school authorities penalized the bully, since she had a record mile long. It was first and only offense made by the young girl in self-defense. Teachers and classmates came to her rescue.

The young girl finally fought back with the same strength she had been attacked, for so long. The results were unimaginable wonderful. This time the girl, whom always was bullied for the longest walked the other way with her head up unashamed. On the other hand, Rose Marie could walk with her head high proud of the new emerged personality. She felt a new person wonderfully satisfied. Quickly, she gained classmates respect lost for so many years.

Never again, did she allow anyone to hurt her inner soul or treat with humiliation. Word spread around like gunfire. The other students needed a bully to lead them, also left her alone. Spanish-speaking students became closer "friends." Rose Marie felt a sense of belong to the school and the city surrounded by new friends.

Dreams of popular once again surged even if it took three years, but finally materialized. Glances of admiration and words of encouragement were the topics for the next days, weeks and the rest of her Senior year. For the first time, in a long time, she felt popular again, just like back home. That was the best standing ovation in itself.

The next day, the newcomer walked into the cafeteria. There was moment of silence. Glances, low whispers, smiles, and sweet phrases followed as she walked slowly by. The world stood still for a moment. Time stopped and Rose Marie made her debut. Chairs pulled out were an invitation to sit next to those that once killed her silently with indifference low tolerance. Rather, she chose to sit with the faithful Hispanic group. They were always supportive and understood her pain. They accepted without question the customs, traditions, or her looks. This time, she had tears of joy instead of sadness, as they all stood up and clapped for an endless moment.

The auditorium became the place to meet and hang out with the new friends. Those lonely times of isolation were finally over. There was a standing ovation in her heart. Every morning, before she left the house, she thanked God for the victory against the bullies. Rose Marie asked God for forgiveness, but could not turn the other side of the cheek. Instead, she thank God for the help to solve the problem, that once overwhelmed the newcomer.

The graduation time came near, Rose Marie's life completely changed. She asked the assigned counselor to help search for the proper colleges. The counselor had to take into consideration her economic circumstances below poverty level and needed a college could afford. The counselor insistently questioned, "Why, she wanted to go to college?" The counselor did not bother to mention the terms "Financial Aid, grant, nor scholarship."

The first choice was Farleigh Dickinson University, one of the most expensive in the area. Actually, Rose Marie had very little information about other universities. Therefore, the perspectives were limited.

She remembered the day at the counselor's office and saw a campus picture, which caught her attention. She felt immediately in love with the beautiful greenery campus. Even though, it was quite out of her league.

Nevertheless, she dreamed about the campus surrounded by many new friends under the huge trees in the poster. In addition, attracted by the illustrious name, Rose Marie applied to William Paterson College in remembrance of the city's inspirational history. The college was accessibly near, so there could be a chance. Those were the two choices recommended to a poor student lived in poverty conditions with a handful dream.

Finally, the acceptance letters came. Sadly, she realized college was out of question at least for the moment, due to money issues. Then, her dreams were put on hold, but for a while. The two colleges were expensive out of reach of the family's income range.

Clearly, Rose Marie remembered the day the first letter arrived. It was from Farleigh Dickinson. They accepted her application for the fall semester. Then, came the second letter from William Paterson College, the long desired acceptance. Bewildered, she read the letters repeatedly.

Then, the father-imposed figure broke the enchantment and stated he could not afford to pay for college tuition. Instead, he insisted to search for a full time job to help with the bills. The news broke her heart, but accepted her destiny.

Every time, she passed by the universities, the aching heart belonged in one of those campuses. She deserved to have an education, like her sister, but for the moment it was denied. It just would take a bit longer to accomplish the college dreams. Rose Marie's dreams were put on hold!

Finally, the day came for the graduate class of 1968. She was thrill to complete all the requirements even under such strenuous circumstances. She was proud of herself. Surprisingly, both parents came to the graduation. Then, she left quietly home, but satisfied after sincere congratulations and sadly good-byes from all new acquired friends.

Surprisingly, the bully came up to the Latina girl and without words, both embraced. Rose Marie had already forgave the young girl who looked for attention in a negative way. Rose Marie knew as a Christian she had to forgive and forget and continue her way through life.

There was nothing to celebrate, no parties, just a great sense of relief to be out. Deep inside, there was no sadness in her heart. The young girl was happy to leave behind, the gates of hell, as Rose Marie harshly joked and referred to the school. Rose Marie felt satisfied to know she conquered the hostile environment and subdue her enemies by the grace of God.

Then, Rose Marie obtained the ultimate goal graduation, even against the odds. an accomplishment for a standing ovation!

Because the Sovereign Lord helps me, "I will not be disgraced. Therefore have I set my face like flint, and I know I will not be put to shame." Isaiah 50:7

Afterwards, she went to work in a nearby factory assembled lamps. The hands full of blisters, glue and cuts earned enough money to bring alive the dream which simmered in her mind. She worked full time and studied part time in Jersey City State College, then transferred to Montclair State College. The commute to work and college went on for several years.

At Montclair State College, she met wonderful fascinating professors that helped the girl focus in her college carrier. The professors channeled her energies into the right direction gave the strength and courage to go on. Eventually, returned home to the beloved island finished her college career in The University of Puerto Rico, with the help of a scholarship. Finally, Rose Marie graduated with high honors and continued schooling achieved a Master Degree, another standing ovation. In addition, took acting classes and focused on director stage plays. The skills learned were later used in life when Rose Marie wrote and directed plays for theaters fulfilling the emptiness of not becoming an actor after all, but escalating into a whole new level.

Overall, years later had the opportunity to become a play-writer and saw theater performances from her plays! Years later, Rose Marie among many things became a Christian playwright. Rose Marie had the personal satisfaction to invite the beloved actress Marta Romero to one of the Christian production presented at the island's prestigious theater.

Rose Marie spoke to the famous actress who mostly kept to herself. She heard the lovely voice almost a whisper come from behind closed doors. *Martha* made excuses for not opening the door. Rose Marie introduced herself as the playwright, director and producer of the play, *"Birth of an Enterpriser,"* (*Nacimiento de un Empresario*) once lifetime opportunity presented on stage.

Rose Marie spoke to the beloved actress cordially invited to the presentation with front row seat reservation. The actress politely promised to come to the performance opening night, but unfortunately never showed up. Instead, the seat remained empty. The idealized image faded quickly away with great disappointment, but still deep admiration. Afterwards, Rose Marie heard comments deducted the actress really wanted to be remembered young and beautiful. Therefore, she concealed her face from fans and friends.

Finally, Rose Marie came to terms with herself, overcame the feelings of empty phrases once echoed in her mind. The Glory and the thanks be given to God!

"Search me, Oh God, and know my heart: test me and know my anxious thoughts. See if there is any offensive way in me, and lead me in the way everlasting." Psalm 139: 23-24

●●●

Chapter 17

THE NEW SILK CITY

*"The Lord is good to those who wait for him,
to the soul who seek Him."*
Lamentations 3:23

Occasionally, Rose Marie had the urge to visit the city. She wanted to witness where the ruins of her young girl's heart took place, but also the rise and accomplishments of dreams. She went back to visit the fast pace city and seemed a charming wonderful place. She learned to love Silk City with all its goodness and badness it had to offer.

Still, Rose Marie felt a special attraction in the greatest powerful waterfalls, at one time smoothed her pain. The nature connection in the brick city always bonded with the girl. Rose Marie went often to the places she drew strength to survive. She felt part of her life, were left behind in Paterson. A place, she hated at first then loved dearly.

Nowadays, the Latina girl goes for a different reason. She likes to snap shots for the photograph collection on the Great Falls. Silk city will always be her second home. The place, she matured into womanhood.

She learned to recognize the glorious history and embraced the city. Rose Marie was proud of Silk City's remarkable history; the first finest industrial center, in the United States. The Great Falls at the

Passaic River are the second highest in water volume, next to the biggest at Niagara Falls, in Canada. In 1974, the Great Falls area were an important role in Mary Ellen Kramer's life; the wife of Mayor Lawrence Pat Kramer. The mayor's wife dedicated her time and efforts to promote the preservation of city's historical sites of the Great Falls Historic Trails. Mrs. Kramer, with a strong sense of history, was responsible for the invitation to President Gerald Ford to visit the city. Hooray, for Mrs. Mary Ellen Kramer!

In June 6, 1976, President Ford came officially to designate the area as National Historic Landmark, for all Americans to enjoy. Rose Marie lived a few blocks away from the waterfall. She heard about the President's visit to the Great Falls and stood in front of the home in the eminent path of the Presidential route to proudly waved a huge Puerto Rican flag in support of the visit. Excited, without thoughts or the consequences, she ran alongside the Presidential car for a few seconds, enough to slow them up.

Then, she got a more direct personal salute and a smile from the President himself, something the guards disliked, and gently pushed her away. Still, she remembers his wonderful smile and wave back. Therefore, unintentionally the Latina girl captured the front headlines in the local newspaper; The Herald News, the next morning. Again, it was better than a standing ovation back home!

Afterwards, the outside structure of the High School was remodel. The structure no longer looked scary and harsh, like years ago. The old, musty building seemed harmless and less intimidated, but always felt cold. The school's spirit lived in her heart even at faraway lands. She felt sorry the school never gave her a true chance demonstrate her talents.

Despite, those dreadful years deep inside, she had the urged to go back to visit the High School, but only drove past the building. Never again, Rose Marie went inside the marble building of the High School. Sometimes, she gets the urge to see and touch the marble walls. The pain and misery from those teen years of the inexperienced immature High School days remained encrusted inside those walls. If only those walls could talk!

It was something in her wanted to go inside, and see those marble walls that crushed those youthful years. She traveled in time with closed eyes and wondered down the lonely cold corridors. She wanted to touch those cold white hallways, perhaps to reflect upon them.

She wondered from time to time, if the auditorium used as a hide place for others. Rose Marie wanted to sit on those comfortable cushioned chairs one more time, and shout, *"Hey, I'm here. Thanks for your protection that made me invisible in my worst moments."*

She wanted to shout to bullies and others, *"You could not destroy or devour me, I'm still here!"* Maybe one day...she will be invited as a speaker to let others know her story of survival during High School years! Nevertheless, still carried around the precious miniature diploma and safeguards the original, as a treasure. She would love to see Mrs. Lopez, but married a few years later changed her name.

She will always remain a special teacher in her heart. Indeed, would like to tell her, despite the pain and suffer, made it in the world.

Thanks to the love of God, Rose Marie kept thoughts of her childhood memories and special moments in her heart. At times, Rose Marie felt like a real Patersonian without forgetting her roots.

Ironically, Rose Marie became a teacher. It was an easy decision. Perhaps, Rose Marie was influenced by the inner soft-spoken voice, which brought tranquility to her aching broken heart. After all, she became a good decent human being, and strive to be the best teacher ever, reflected in the teaching philosophy and living style. God gave Rose Marie the victory!

Rose Marie got much more than a standing ovation from back home! Rose Marie won the highest award as a teacher given in Puerto Rico called the *"Teacher of Excellence"* in year 2000, a proclamation signed by *Maria Sila Calderon,* first female Governor of the island, made history again!

By the way, she became, "English as a Second Language teacher" served at an inner city school, Bronx, New York, and lived nearby the Paterson Falls for the duration of the contract. The position gave the best opportunity to show students a positive difference in their lives. They were valuables first to God, then to their family and community.

She taught them the English language, and then to believe in themselves. First, because social barriers can be broken down, no matter what, with help of the all Mighty.

She let them know dreams were possible and could be accomplish to the fullest. Like Mae Jemison, the first African –American woman in space in 1992 once said, *"Never let people with limited imagination limit you from your dreams."*

She wanted the students to remember as someone who really cared! She stayed alert as a teacher, looked out for those students, which might show signs of suffer and frustration in the new country. She became the teacher who looked out for others that might have their world crumbled and smashed from right under their feet. Just, like she lived a long time ago. As a teacher, is vigilant, so it will not happen again!

In 2005, the ovation continued in the New York schools system. Rose Marie won the award, *"Educator of the Week."* An award sponsored by major Spanish Television Network Channel 41, *"Univision,"* in conjunction with New York Lottery. The award celebrated educators, "going the extra mile and put students first." She has professional licenses, from several states: New Jersey, New York, six from Puerto Rico; including Principal, and finally Florida, where she resided. Indeed, God is good!

She had time to heal and recovered from those awful teenage years, and goes back to visit and stays near the waterfalls in "Silk City," Paterson. She made many good friends. Throughout the years, those friends have made a positive difference in her life and changed the outlook upon the city. She is not being able stay away and shares the mystical powers of waterfalls with all.

Silk City

Wonderful growing city vibrates with each project, new industry, lavish commerce, new housing and new people aboard. The Historic Museum enhances the valuable historical relics information that helped mold country's economy. In the Museum and in the historic area are the evidences and the testimony on restored buildings, surroundings, and important documents for all to see. Mostly, the city uniquely possesses valuable natural resources, the most beautiful waterfalls during all four seasons. The city celebrates cultural mixtures in citywide festivals, celebrated in the Historic Trails. However, most of all, the city possess valuable human resources, which are people from different cultural backgrounds.

Nowadays, people learned to accept cultural diversity. The city has accepted diversity because it enhances communities cultural richness and learning experiences. They learned to respect who sacrificed first to open doors with their lives, hard workers, sweat, blood, tears and spirit, for others to enjoy, also. We all learned from each other passionate desires that take to survive, and make it in the world. If, you can survive Silk City, you can survive anywhere!

Time changed the outlook of the city and worthily mention. Recently, a Puerto Rican made history in Paterson, when he became the first Spanish mayor elected in the city with his slogan, "Proud to be a Patersonian." Eventually, *Jose "Joey" Torres* will go down in history as the first Hispanic, from Puerto Rico, 44th Mayor conquered the field of politics, in *Silk City*. Names, written in special places next to the outstanding personalities of Maria Magda; the first Puerto Rican council member. Also, Sonia Rosado council member and first Hispanic woman elected freeholder; a personal friend of Rose Marie. In process are other names, like Nelly Pou, next to many Rivera's, Rodriguez, Perez, the Gonzalez, the Martinez...and many more which are in the process to create their own place in history and add to the sidelines of the great historical city.

Newcomers are always welcome to enter the city limits. The beauty of the waterfalls seduces them with its powerful sounds. The falls beauty quickly hypnotizes all. The city has an open gentle invitation to stay and try the game of life, to see if they can survive its thrust! Alternatively, as once Rose Marie, you will be also subdued at the mist of Silk City. People from all over will always come to see the Great Waterfalls no matter, if it overflows Passaic River or scarcely without water.

Remember the silkworm analogy, from ugliness ruins comes within something valuable, good and beautiful! It is all inside, just let it loose! Remember love fully and passionately, whatever you decide to become, as you place your own footprints in history helped by the powerful love of God! Only, He has the power to turn bad things into good. Love God above anything and give him first place! Nevertheless and most of all, be good to yourself, so you can be good to others!

"God is my strength and power and He makes my way perfect."2 Samuel 22"33

Therefore, I shall not want...in Silk City, or elsewhere! God bless! Adios! Good-bye! Bon Jour! Arrividelche! Sayonara! ●●●

Silk City

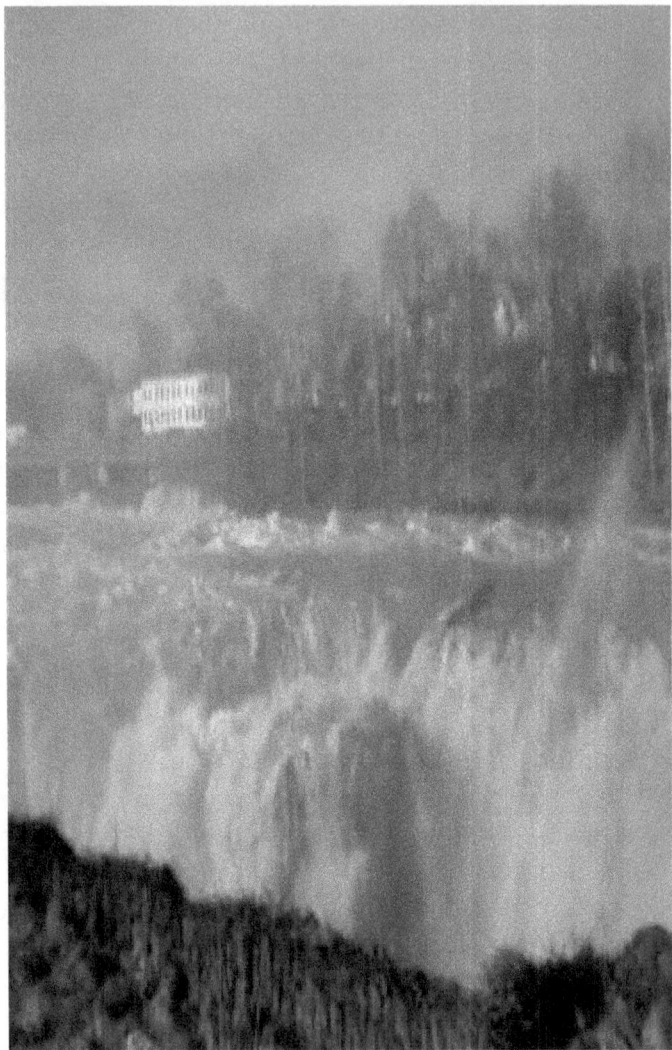

After the rain, will always see the rainbow!

Poetry

THEN and NOW

Used to say country,
Now say city.
Used to walk
Now run at gigantic steps.
Used to cry,
Now laugh, about it all
Used to see crystal grin,
Now, envision the future green.
I used to ask, why?
Now say, why not!
Used to think time languish on,
Now reflect time has fleet too swift.
Used to say later, perhaps, then,
But, now is when!
Used to say never again,
Now, always try over again.
Used to fear the unfamiliar,
Now, I know can survive all,
even the unknown!

WHEN I WAS A CHILD

(Memories of dear grandma…Aleja)

When a child, I slept with
Sweet Grandma Aleja,
Without moving an inch,
Or else would freeze.
She was cuddly
Like a fuzzy bear,
Ready to mush fears away.

When a child, I walked
Inside her nightly rope,
With my arms gripped,
Around her waist.
As she became my lifesaver,
In an open sea,
From the freezing apartment 7-C.

When a child,
I took giant steps,
To follow granny around
Where ever she bend.
She turned to boil coffee
And toasted bread,
For early working birds.

Silk City

When a child, I kept warm
In her arm,
Close to her soft skin,
Heard sizzled bacon on stove,
The only heat source.
Until, who knows when?
The landlord last resource,
Send the heat perhaps around,
Ten o'clock or more.

When a child, I tried keep warm
Yes, to keep warm I tried
With her breath, I thought,
Then, I dared my hands
Touched steam boiled water,
Vapors clouded windows,
Invaded my breath, soul and kitchen, too.

When a child, I moved tugged
Inside her embraced bosom,
Until, I felt safely warm
Enough to touch my nose.
While, she carefully moved
With the extra cargo, blindly held
Until surely the temperature rose!

As a child, I let my face,
Touch her soft skin.
I felt my fingers and toes soar,
Then, I felt warm again,
But waited the final blow
For the cold clunk radiator
And coughed the final roar!

[143]

When a child, I acted
Like a child.
Now, grown
nothing can replace
The warmest love,
from dearest granny!
When she carried me
around her waist.
As, I held tightly,
So, I would not freeze
To death surely,
In the freezing apartment 7-C!

About the Author

Brunilda Milan was born on the beautiful island Puerto Rico, lived many years in Paterson, New Jersey. Currently, she is a teacher in Florida; the Sunshine State. She has a great passion for writing. Once, she asked a famous writer, how to know when you are a writer? Cleverly, she responded, *"When you can't eat, or sleep thinking, what will be the next story."*

The author's main goal is to perpetuate childhood and teenage memories for future generations to learn lessons from memorable experiences enriched with historical facts. The books are realistic historical fictional stories with a sense of history in each. Also reflects taste for poetry with the abundance in similes and metaphors.

Silk City (2012) based on teenage high school experience developed at sidelines historical city Paterson, where she compares the island to the city.

Rediscover the Island of Puerto Rico; (Feb 2009) is about a young girl visited the island for the first time as a child then as a teenager. She discovered hidden treasures in the history and illustrious' people contributions.

The Case of the Missing Mon, (July 2009) is true story of a woman disappearance for eight years missed only by daughters who never gave up and looked for their mom. A case treated by authorities as one more missing person in a big city.

Paper Love, (2012), romance story of young girl's broken heart by someone just wanted to obtain citizenship threw the innocence of love.

Children Stories from the Heart, (May 2009) a book for children to comprehend English, while reading, a must for those learning the language.

On the other hand, written in Spanish:

Sin Tapujos, (2007) (Without Deceive) is a young boy in drugs, the manipulations, symptoms, and road to recovery.

"Los Cuentos de Antaño de Papá," written right after the father's death in 2008. (The Old Times Stories from Father) Treasured stories told by the

father on how things were in the past while he grew as an adolescent.

The books can be obtained threw amazon.com, click books, then write brunilda Milan or website: brunildamilan.com. Hope, all enjoyed the stories, as much as, I enjoyed to write them.

Remember, there is always a story inside of you.

The writings are with love from the heart!

"Come, let us sing for joy to the Lord; let us shout to the Rock of our salvation." Psalms 95:1

Therefore... I SHALL NOT WANT...

Silk City

Books are available on line
click books
then write brunilda milan

For comments or workshops on self-esteem
and motivational talks contact:
brunildamilan.com

brunildamilan@gmail.com
Milan Publisher
Biblical Scriptures--- taken from
Reina Valera Bible (revised edition)